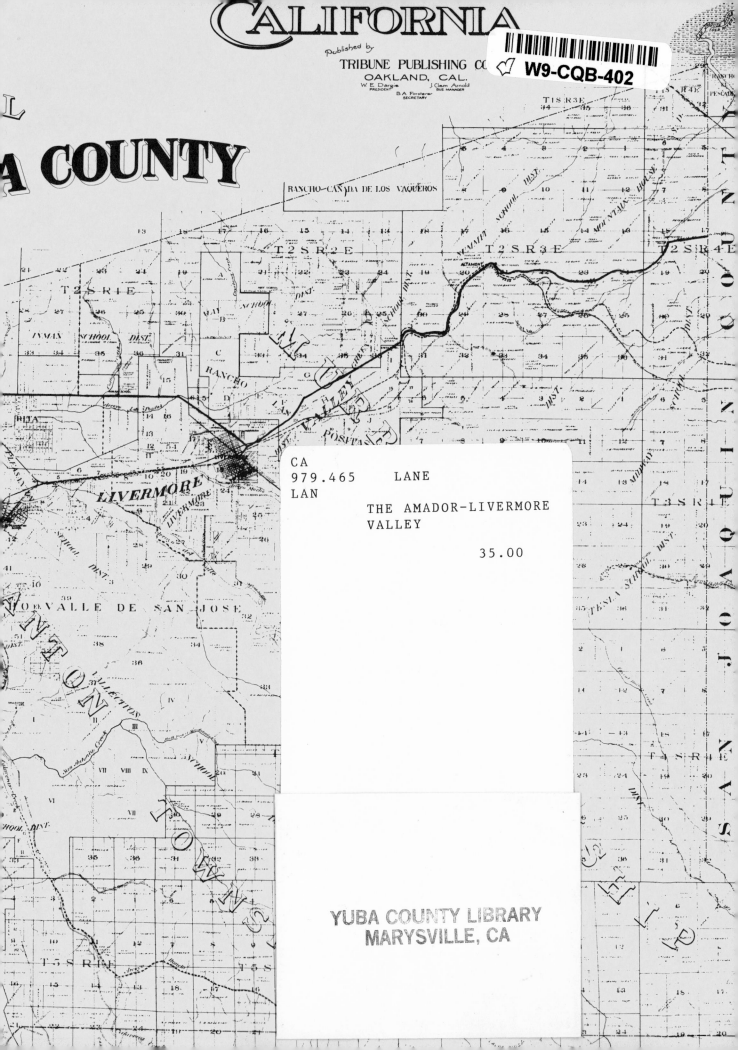

CALIFORNIA

Published by

TRIBUNE PUBLISHING CO
OAKLAND, CAL.

W.E. Dargie   J. Clem Arnold
PRESIDENT   BUS. MANAGER

B.A. Forsterer
SECRETARY

A COUNTY

The Museum

Published by

Amador-Livermore Valley Historical Society

603 Main Street
Pleasanton, California 94566
(415) 462-2766

The Amador-Livermore Valley

A PICTORIAL HISTORY

BOB and PAT LANE

Design by Sharon Varner Moyer

THE DONNING COMPANY
PUBLISHERS
NORFOLK/VIRGINIA BEACH

Dedicated to the continued work of the Amador-Livermore Valley Historical Society, the Livermore Heritage Guild, and the Dublin Historical Preservation Association.

The Donning Company/Publishers
Norfolk/Virginia Beach

The Donning Company/Publishers
5659 Virginia Beach Boulevard
Norfolk, Virginia 23502

Edited by Veronica Kirk
Richard A. Horwege, Senior Editor

Library of Congress Cataloging-in-Publication Data

Lane, Bob, 1925-
   The Amador-Livermore Valley.

   Bibliography: p.
   Includes index.
   1. Livermore Valley (Calif.)—History—Pictorial works. 2. Livermore
Valley (Calif.)—Description and travel—1981-   —Views. I. Lane,
Pat, 1931-   . II. Title.
F868.A3L35   1988   979.4'65   88-18918
ISBN 0-89865-722-9

Printed in the United States of America

Contents

*Abandoned May School in the northern
part of the Amador-Livermore Valley
opened in the 1870s to serve area farm
families. It now is a dying monument in
the dry, barren hills. ALVHS Archives.*

Foreword

In a short span of years we will be at the end of the twentieth century and at the beginning of the twenty-first. The time is here to reflect and ponder the questions, "Who are we, and what are we?" The contents of the following pages attempt to give a glimpse of what we are, a demonstration of our former life-style and our accomplishments. We and our forbears have striven for almost two centuries to make Amador-Livermore Valley the place of good life and satisfying human experience. The pioneers of the past inspired us and set our minds to accomplish what we have today.

The first Europeans to explore here in the eighteenth century saw a rich and verdant wilderness with elk, deer, bear, and many other creatures, and inhabited by primitive tribes of low cultural development. Mission San Jose was established in 1797 and made this valley and its surrounding hills their cattle pasture. The first European settlement was at Dublin, the San Ramon of Jose Amador, where, as early as 1823, items needed by the coastal settlers were being made. The workers were mostly Christian Indians, and their reason for being here was to have their manufacturing safe from marauding pirates along the coast. Californians didn't know until about 1828 that they had become a province of the new state of Mexico.

A few years later, 1834, the Mission of San Jose closed, and this valley was divided into four ranchos: Rancho San Ramon of Amador, Rancho El Valle de San Jose of the Bernals, Rancho Santa Rita del Valle de San Jose of Pacheco, and Rancho Las Positas del Valle de San Jose of Robert Livermore and Noriega. Cattle had been the main interest of the mission fathers, and so it remained the interest of the ranchos.

The war with Mexico ended in 1848, and we became a territory of the United States of America. The gold rush of that same year brought people from all parts of the country and the world. In 1850 we became the state of California. Gold was diminished, and settlers turned their interests to the land, in particular the coastal and inner valley lands, settling where they chose without concern regarding ownership.

A period of uncertainty and confusion of land titles followed, and in this time there emerged some pioneers who should be remembered. At Dublin, the valley's first town which grew at the intersection of two important stage lines, we commemorate the names of Murray, Fallon, and Dougherty and also John Green. These men donated land and encouraged commerce, but the prosperity of this Irish community was short-lived. The opening of the Western Pacific Railroad, later the Central Pacific, brought commercial centers along the line to Pleasanton and Livermore, causing the business people of Dublin to establish themselves at new centers that offered greater opportunity and growth.

At Pleasanton, the founders of the town were John Kottinger, an Austrian, and Joshua Neal, both recipients of land through marriage to a Bernal daughter. At Livermore, Alphonso Ladd had established Laddsville on a stage line route which was later served by the railroad. In 1870 Laddsville burned, and most of the businesses moved west into William Mendenhall's new town of Livermore. Like his contemporaries at Pleasanton, Mendenhall planned his town and filed a plot map with the County of Alameda in 1869, the same year that the first train came through the valley.

Livermore experienced the quickest development and became the largest commercial and shipping center. In Pleasanton, John Kottinger was the first justice of the peace and from that center came law and order. Livermore, unlike Pleasanton where water was in never-ending supply, needed water to be brought from a distant source to supply the growing needs of the commercial district. We credit John Aylward with this accomplishment, bringing water from Cedar Mountain to the town in redwood flumes and distributing it to customers through redwood pipes. He called his enterprise the Livermore Spring Water Company. In the 1890s Dennis Bernal lit the town with electricity, later selling his company to John Aylward who then named the complex the Livermore Water and Power Company.

In the field of education, one of the most important

institutions of all times, Lilly Harris, is remembered in Pleasanton. Livermore recalls Miss Weeks, the first teacher, then Emma Smith, and later Vera Dutcher Crane at the elementary school and Miss May Nissen at Livermore High School, who gave our schools a very high scholastic record in the 1930s and 1940s. There are other names too numerous to mention in all fields of community development. We remember these people with fondness and marvel at their accomplishments.

From a forest inhabited by primitive tribes we have become a valley of high modern development and technology that the pioneers would not have imagined. Our forests have long since gone for the building of other communities and for fuel, even the sycamores to decorate fine furniture. The land was cleared for agriculture but is now covered with housing and business establishments. Changes have made the valley unrecognizable for the first pioneers, and the deer and elk have been pushed to the highest hills. But this is the price that is paid for man's progress. We hope that what we are doing at the present time will provide a suitable and happy environment for the generations of the future.

—Herbert L. Hagemann, Jr.
1988

Acknowledgments

The Board of Directors of Amador Valley Savings is to be recognized and commended for its interest as sponsors to enable the first printing to be done and the Amador-Livermore Valley Historical Society Board of Directors for showing continued interest to make the second printing possible.

We would also like to give special recognition to Herbert L. "Herb" Hagemann of Livermore for his keen interest in local history, fascinating anecdotes, broad knowledge of valley names, dates, and places, and willingness to share in this pictorial effort about early history in the Amador-Livermore Valley. And thanks also go to Mr. Hagemann's mother Edna Kottinger Hagemann for her alert commentary.

Photographs play an obvious role in a pictorial, the following sources being instrumental in supplying the majority of prints used: Amador-Livermore Historical Society Archives (Dagmar Fulton), Livermore Heritage Guild (Barbara Bunshah), Dublin Historical Preservation Association (Virginia Bennett), John Sarboraria (photo collection), and Mrs. Pauline Dopking (photo collection of her late husband, Elliott Dopking).

Sharing family and business photo treasures and information were Barry Schrader, Robert and Elaine Koopmann, Janet Newton, Donna Kamp McMillion, E. H. and Gloria Stahlnecker, Sally Bystroff, William Apperson, Geraldine Ratti Nerton, Julie Eckroat, James Trimingham, Warren Harding, Bob Philcox, Peter Bailey, Bill Owens, Robert and Freida Steffenauer, Shirley Casterson, Bernice Delgado, Bev Ales, Robert Butler, Ralph Arbeloa, Joann Hendrix, Betty Winn Kozlowski, Betty Erker, Harold and Evelyn Moller, William H. Gale, Ed Kinney, Bob Graham, Cotton Heitman, J. D. "Bud" Thornton, and Bev Davis. Close family support came from Ruth Thomas, Donald J. Lane, Thomas M. Lane, Laurie F. Stull, and Chloe and Annica.

From the ALVHS Museum we are indebted to Mary Jane Kuony, Ann Lewis, Cynthia Ostle, Pat Connolly, and Dagmar Fulton for archival help. Information was gleaned mainly from a small mountain of books, pamphlets, papers, news clippings, and other records with this volunteer help. And for making all of those black and white photo prints, thanks goes to Bob Philis of Robert Thomas Photography of Pleasanton and Ron Suttora of Livermore.

Pat and I would also like to thank ourselves for saving twenty years worth of newspaper photographs and negatives, several of which are in this text, and for preserving with two cameras and a copy stand to create new negatives from donated prints from individuals and from the archives of the three historical groups in the valley. We are extremely pleased to have been able to donate our time and expertise to this project, one which we hope enables a "new" population in the valley to understand who and what we are because we now know somewhat of where we have been, and perhaps we can determine where we are going.

—Bob and Pat Lane
1989

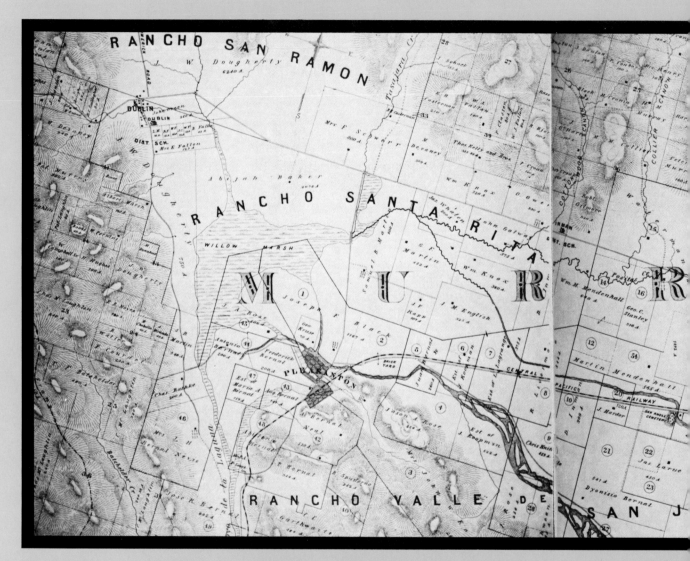

The Amador-Livermore Valley is seen in the Thompson and West Historical Atlas *map of Alameda County as published in 1878. ALVHS Archives*

Chapter 1

The First Settlers in the Amador-Livermore Valley

In 1824 Mission San Jose granted Jose Maria Amador four square leagues of land (called Rancho San Ramon) in order to manufacture blankets, soap, saddles, harness, and other goods. He received title to the land in 1834 when the mission was to be secularized. The inland manufacturing escaped pirate raids and by 1837 as many as 150 local Native American Indians and Mexicans were helping with the manufacturing and the farming. He built a two-story adobe house and other buildings near today's Dublin-San Ramon area.

Amador's success was seen in his ownership of 300-400 horses, 13,000-14,000 cattle, and 3,000-4,000 sheep.

Others began to arrive in the valley. In 1837 Robert Livermore and Jose Noriega purchased Rancho Las Positas. Other ranchos were Santa Rita (Jose Pacheco) and in 1839 Rancho Valle de San Jose, granted to Juan Pablo and Agostin Bernal, Antonio Sunol, and Antonio Maria Pico. Antonio was the first settler in the Sunol area, and married a Bernal daughter. Headquarters for the rancho were at Alisal (Pleasanton) with a major domo supervising the land and the cattle and horse raising.

Robert Livermore arrived in 1837 on Rancho Las Positas and married Josefa Higuera Molina the next year. He was successful in raising cattle, horses, and sheep on his settlement which was the farthest inland among the ranchos.

Agostin Bernal began an adobe in 1848 near Alisal (the cottonwood groves, originally named in 1772 by Spanish soldiers). Juan Pablo Bernal was also living in Alisal in an adobe in what is thought to be the present site

Jose Maria Amador. ALVHS Archives

of the Amador Valley Joint Union High School. Agostin built a small horse racetrack in 1860 (now the site of the Alameda County Fairgrounds).

Austrian native John W. Kottinger filed for citizenship in New Orleans in 1846 and completed his naturalization in San Francisco in 1850. He was the first American in the Amador-Livermore Valley, arriving in Alisal in 1851 to raise cattle and build an adobe home (demolished in 1930) and a barn (restored) near the Arroyo Del Valle (now 200 Ray Street, Pleasanton). He married Juan Bernal's daughter Refugia (Maria Refugia Agosta de Bernal). The Kottinger adobe home site was near Ray Street but to the west toward Main Street.

According to several sources, when Kottinger was the judge in Alisal, his adobe was used as the courtroom. An underground passageway led to his adobe barn to the east, through which prisoners were taken to be locked in a cell in a corner of the barn.

In 1863, Kottinger gave land parcels for small sums. He drew a map for the town of Alisal in 1867, renaming it Pleasonton in honor of his good friend Alfred Pleasonton, a general in the Civil War. A clerking error caused the Post Office application to come back from Washington, D.C., as Pleasanton and the spelling stuck.

Also in 1863 Joshua A. Neal, who had land next to Kottinger's, completed a survey and sold building lots on the county road now known as Main Street. Kottinger did a second survey in 1869 to align his property with the Western Pacific Railroad right of way.

Saint Mary, Saint John, and central Main Streets were locations for the earliest homes and businesses. The original Pleasanton Hotel, destroyed by fire and never rebuilt, was located at the corner of Saint Mary and Main. Pictures and information appear later in this chapter.

In the northern portion of the Amador-Livermore Valley Jeremiah Fallon and wife Eleanor (Michael Murray sister) settled in Dublin following an attempt at gold mining in the Mother Lode in 1849. In 1850 Michael and

Jose Narcisco Sunol, son of Antonio, built an adobe near the town of Sunol, just east of what is today the entrance to the Water Temple of the San Francisco Water System.

On the night of January 6, 1845, about 220 men under the command of John A. Sutter camped at Sunol's adobe on their way from Sacramento to the pueblo of Los Angeles to fight for colonization of Northern California. ALVHS Archives

Robert Livermore and wife Josefa.
ALVHS Archives

Jeremiah bought one thousand acres from Amador and began ranching. The next year James Dougherty and William Glaskin bought ten thousand acres from Amador, who in 1852 sold the rancho to Dougherty. The settlement became known variously as Amador, Dublin, and Dougherty's Station.

In 1857 John Green purchased Murray's share, and by the next year more people were lured to the valley to farm. Edwin Horan, William Murray, John Martin, F. Knapp, and Robert Graham all rented Dougherty land, hoping to raise bumper crops of grain.

Fallon and Murray donated land for and helped build the first school (Murray School) and the first church (Saint Raymond's Catholic Church in 1859). In the 1860s the crossroads at Dublin was a thriving center as a stage-coach stop with hotels, a general store, harness and blacksmith shops, and other businesses. But completion of the railroad through the valley in 1869 ended the prosperous Dublin period with development shifting mainly to Livermore, and to a lesser degree, Pleasanton.

Two main roads crossed at Dublin. The east-west route has been known at different times as Dublin Road, Stockton Road, Lincoln Highway, Highway 50, and currently as the 580 Freeway. The north-south route came through Dublin from the Mt. Diablo area as San Ramon Road and wound its way through Pleasanton and the hills to Sunol, then on to Mission San Jose.

Alphonso Ladd built a home, a hotel, and a livery stable on Stockton Road immediately north (East First Street and Junction Avenue) of what is now the

Agostin Bernal. ALVHS Archives

13

John W. Kottinger. Dopking photo

This early map of Pleasanton was published in 1878. ALVHS Archives, Thompson and West Historical Atlas

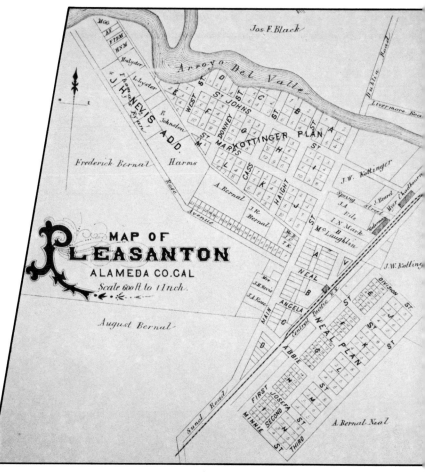

city of Livermore. A fire in 1870 burned Ladsville (also spelled Laddsville) and business moved into the newly forming town of Livermore. Ladd never recovered from the disaster.

Prompted by the arrival of the railroad, William Mendenhall laid out the first plan for a new town in 1869. He renamed his town after old friend Robert Livermore, who had died in 1858. Mendenhall also donated land for the first railroad depot, a school, a church, and parks.

Livermore grew more in 1875 when A. J. McLeod plotted another section of city on the eastern edge of Mendenhall's plan. Almost immediately Alexander Esden filed for a Northern Addition, thus forming a three-part central core from which the town in later years developed in all directions.

In the 1880s many vineyards were planted in the general valley and wineries were built. Various sources list as many as two hundred vineyards and/or wineries oper-

ating during those years. Coal mines, brickyards, a fuse works for explosives, and other mining developed in the late 1800s but most of these activities were discontinued shortly after the turn of the century.

The town of Pleasanton was incorporated in 1894 with a population of about five hundred. Agriculture and cattle and horse raising continued as the main generators of income until the 1940s when World War II brought the military north of Pleasanton and when the 1950s brought Lawrence Livermore Laboratory and Sandia to Livermore. Ten years later General Electric Vallecitos was built in the hills near the two communities.

In the pages that follow, a pictorial sequence will show much of the development in the Amador-Livermore Valley through early businesses, agriculture and wine making, homes and architecture, industries, churches and schools, a few major events, medical facilities, railroads, and the influence of the military.

The Jose Joaquin Bernal and Maria Josefa Sanchez marriage resulted in twelve children, half of whom had off-spring who married and populated the Amador-Livermore Valley. Old timers say that at one time almost everyone in the valley was related to a Bernal.

The composite picture shows many of these early pioneers: (1) Maria Castro y Feliz, (2) Rafaela Feliz y Bernal, (3) Maria Refugia Agosta Bernal y Kottinger, (4) John William Kottinger, (5) Eva T. Kottinger, (9) Mathias Kottinger, (10) Martha R. Kottinger, (10 in corner) John David Kottinger, (11) Guadalupe Bernal, (12) Juan Pablo Bernal, (13) Antonio Maria Pico, (14) John David Kottinger, (15) William Bradford Kottinger, (16) Alfred E. Kottinger, (17) Herman Mark Kottinger, and (18) Rosa Kottinger. ALVHS Archives-Hagemann Collection

Juan Pablo Bernal

Their marriage resulted in five children, three of whom produced offspring who went on to establish leading families in

Rafaela Feliz y Bernal

the Amador-Livermore Valley. Refer to the abbreviated chart which follows. ALVHS Archives

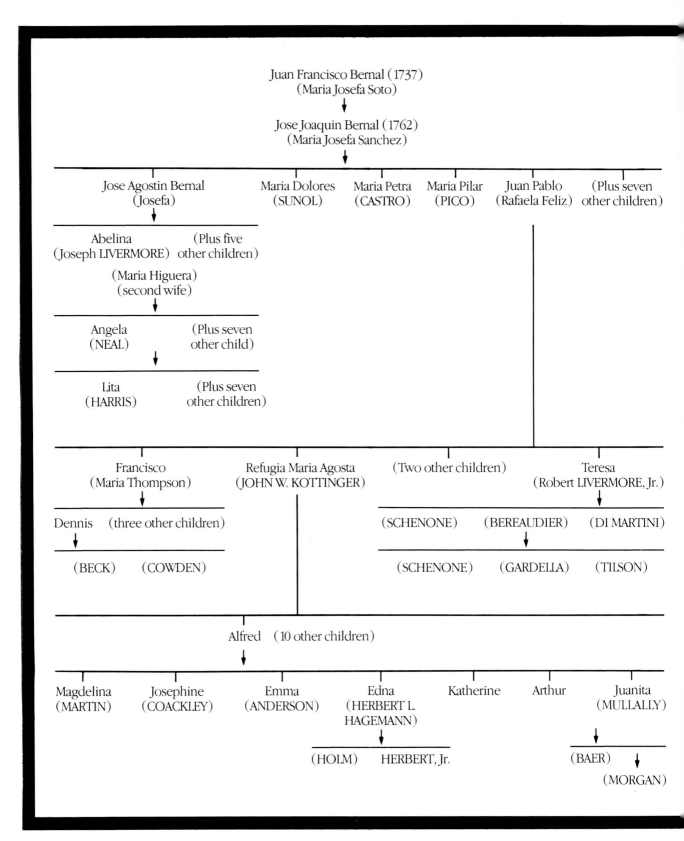

Juan Francisco Bernal (1737)
(Maria Josefa Soto)

↓

Jose Joaquin Bernal (1762)
(Maria Josefa Sanchez)

↓

| Jose Agostin Bernal (Josefa) | Maria Dolores (SUNOL) | Maria Petra (CASTRO) | Maria Pilar (PICO) | Juan Pablo (Rafaela Feliz) | (Plus seven other children) |

↓ (under Jose Agostin Bernal)

Abelina
(Joseph LIVERMORE)   (Plus five other children)

(Maria Higuera)
(second wife)

Angela
(NEAL)   (Plus seven other child)

↓

Lita
(HARRIS)   (Plus seven other children)

| Francisco (Maria Thompson) | Refugia Maria Agosta (JOHN W. KOTTINGER) | (Two other children) | Teresa (Robert LIVERMORE, Jr.) |

Dennis   (three other children)

↓

(BECK)   (COWDEN)

(SCHENONE)   (BEREAUDIER)   (DI MARTINI)

↓

(SCHENONE)   (GARDELLA)   (TILSON)

Alfred   (10 other children)

↓

| Magdelina (MARTIN) | Josephine (COACKLEY) | Emma (ANDERSON) | Edna (HERBERT L. HAGEMANN) | Katherine | Arthur | Juanita (MULLALLY) |

↓ (under Edna)

(HOLM)   HERBERT, Jr.

↓ (under Juanita)

(BAER)   ↓

(MORGAN)

This chart of the Jose Joaquin Bernal family, which leads into the Juan Pablo Bernal family here presented, is a greatly shortened genealogical offering showing the importance of one main Amador-Livermore Valley line of descent. The original format of this lineage was prepared by Beverly Ales of Pleasanton from a sketch by Herbert L. Hagemann, Jr., of Livermore.

A quick look at bottom center of the genealogy chart reveals the marriage of Edna Kottinger and Herbert L. Hagemann. Herbert is pictured here as a teenager at the turn of the century when the family paid a visit (probably on a Sunday) to the Koopmann family in Dublin. The families were quite social, and picture taking was a popular pastime. Photo courtesy of Robert Koopmann

As young men are wont to do, Herbert shows off in the buggy by giving Bertha Koopmann a ride. Photo courtesy of Robert Koopmann

Edna Kottinger is seated at center front in this picture of the Livermore High School class of 1910. Buggy rides aside, this is the girl Herbert Hagemann, Sr. married. She resides in the family home on the west end of Olivina Street in Livermore. The three boys are Ray Lamb (left), Hermann Wente (top), and Desmond Teeter (right). Bess Monahan (who married Ernest Wente) is seated next to Edna. LHG Archives

Herbert L. Hagemann, Jr., a pioneer descendant, resides at the family home on Olivina in Livermore. He is active on the Amador-Livermore Valley Historical Society Board and continues a broad interest in community affairs. ALVHS Archives, Peter Bailey Photo

The structures which served Robert Livermore are now gone, but the house built by Antonio Maria Pico near Livermore (now West Olivina) in 1836 remains occupied today. Pico chose spruce lumber from Maine for the original house, even though most others in the area were using adobe blocks. According to the law at that time, he had to make improvements on his share of the Rancho Valle de San Jose.

He sold out to Antonio Sunol in 1842, who sold to Juan Pablo Bernal in 1852. Cattle herders lived in the house during these years. The Martin Mendenhall family became squatters on the land in 1863, later buying it.

August Hagemann bought the house and property in 1896 and resided there until 1906. Herman Ruter rented it until 1916, after which Herbert L. Hagemann, Sr., and Edna Kottinger married and purchased the property.

Edna Hagemann and her son Herbert L. Hagemann, Jr., continue to reside in the original building and additions which were made over the years. Courtesy H. L. Hagemann, Jr.

Joshua A. Neal. ALVHS Archives

Photos are rare of the founders of Dublin. Michael Murray was so influential that he had three schools, a school district, and a township named after him. In 1861 he was elected as the supervisor of Murray Township for Alameda County. DHPA Photo

The J. A. Neal farm and buildings in 1878 as sketched in Thompson and West Historical Atlas. *The house is still standing at Second and Neal streets in Pleasanton. ALVHS Archives*

Only one picture of Jeremiah Fallon was known to have existed, and it was accidently burned. Here is his grave marker in the cemetery behind Old St. Raymond's Church in Dublin. Author Photo

Eleanor Murray Fallon (1815-1896), wife of Jeremiah Fallon. DHPA Photo

Ellen Fallon was born in New Orleans and when only a year old came across the plains in a covered wagon with her brother and parents. She married Wil-liam Tehan in 1865, the first bride to married in Old St. Raymond's Churcl She died at age eighty-three (1845-192 DHPA Photo

James Witt Dougherty 1813-1878. Elizabeth Argyle Dougherty (died in 1887). Dougherty's ten-thousand acres cost $2.20 per acre. After his death, his son sold off much of the land at $64.00 per acre. In 1960 when Volk-McLain began the residential building boom in Dublin the land went for about $2,000.00 per acre. DHPA Photo

William Mendenhall laid out the original plan which began the town of Livermore. Dopking Photo

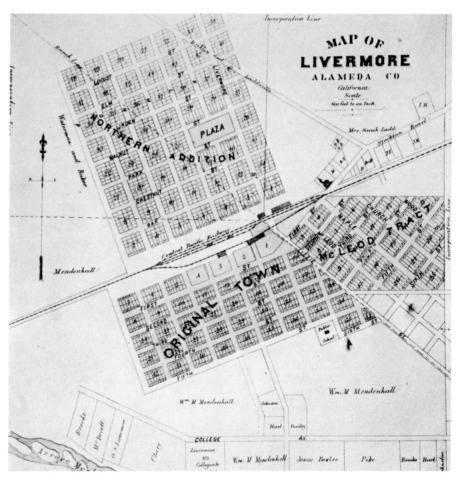

William Mendenhall's "Original Town" of 1869 can be seen at lower center of this map published in 1878. ALVHS Archives, Thompson and West Historical Atlas

In the 1860s Ladsville was a stage stop in the valley. The hamlet boasted a store, a hotel, other businesses, and residences. In 1870 a fire destroyed the buildings and the area never recovered. Business moved to the new town of Livermore, now growing because of the arrival of the railroad. ALVHS Archives

Hotels and Town Businesses for the Agricultural Community

For over a hundred years (1830s-1840s to 1940s-1950s) the greatest influence upon life in the Amador-Livermore Valley was agriculture. The raising and breeding of cattle, sheep, swine, heavy work horses and mules, and sleek race horses dominated, along with bumper crops of barley, wheat, hay, sugar beets, and hops and later vineyards and winemaking.

Serving the rural community at first were stage-stop hamlets such as Altamont, Laddsville, Santa Rita, and Dublin, all on the main road across the valley. As population grew and the railroad arrived (1860s-1870s), the roadside stage stops lost their importance, giving way to rapid development of Livermore and Pleasanton and the resulting centers of community life. Retail businesses (hotels, saloons, cafes, theatres, livery stables, general merchandise and hardware stores, and laundries) and services (banks, doctors, lawyers) mushroomed, as photos in the following chapter illustrate. Still, the emphasis was upon serving the ranchers and farmers of the valley.

Among the most important occupations of the time were the blacksmiths and tinsmiths. In Dublin was Bill Harris, but he moved to Pleasanton when the railroad came through. Also in Pleasanton were H. G. Wells and several more. In Livermore were such names as Aylward,

Beazel, and Holmes who manufactured and repaired wagons, farm machinery, harness, and other leather and metal goods. Aylward is noted for his expertise as a machinist, building a hay press, a steam pumper for the fire department, and a water system. He brought water in redwood flumes from Cedar Mountain to Livermore and then distributed it to customers through redwood pipes.

Early fire departments were primitive at best, but as far back as 1915 a county fire lookout was established on Crane Ridge to help protect the ranchers and farmers. It was sponsored by the Alameda-Contra Costa County Cattlemen's Protective Association. Henrietta Wetmore was one of several residents at the lookout which operated from 1915-1960. John McGlinchey was responsible for starting a county fire department. The original station site is still located on College Avenue in Livermore.

On the pages that follow are businesses and services as they developed in the valley communities: the stage stops, Dublin, Livermore, Pleasanton, and Sunol.

Pleasanton

About five miles to the west of Livermore was the much smaller but growing town of Pleasanton. In 1894 with a population of about five-hundred this hamlet previously called Alisal was incorporated and officially named Pleasanton (see the introduction for the mistaken change in spelling from Pleasonton).

From the mid 1850s to the late 1930s the town grew to about twelve-hundred. During World War II and the later 1940s the population doubled due to the influx of the military at Camp Parks three miles north of town across the highway. In the early 1950s when the Lawrence Livermore Laboratory, Sandia, and G. E. Vallecitos, came into the area, the population grew to almost six-thousand in a short ten-year period.

By 1890 Pleasanton was famous for thoroughbred horses, the original training and racing track having been developed by Agostin Bernal for his Spanish horses. By 1900 the track had been lengthened to a mile. The complex today is the modern Alameda County Fairgrounds. In 1869 the Central Pacific Railroad (Southern Pacific) laid tracks through Pleasanton and south toward Sunol and then west through Niles Canyon and into the Bay Area (see the previous section for the Western Pacific in 1910).

Stage Stops

Stockton Road came through the hills east of the Amador-Livermore Valley, allowing horse-drawn stages and wagons to pass. One of the businesses to thrive in the sparse and forlorn hills was the Summit Hotel at Altamont Pass. This photo taken in the 1920s indicates the spartan existence there. LHG Archives

24

A few miles further west on the Stockton Road was a small settlement similar to Ladsville, which was called Santa Rita and was another stage stop with a store and a blacksmith. The Santa Rita Market wagon shown here may have been a delivery vehicle for the hop fields or simply a door-to-door vendor in the Pleasanton area in the 1880s. ALVHS Archives

John Green opened a general merchandise store at the crossroads in Dublin in the 1850s. It, along with other businesses, thrived as the main stagecoach stop until the coming of the Central Pacific Railroad through Livermore and Pleasanton in 1869 and the Western Pacific in 1910 doomed this center of commerce. Shown here is Green's store, later the Nielsen and Cronin General Store, around 1914. ALVHS Archives

Dublin businesses continued to survive. Here is another view of the Green Store in the 1920s. ALVHS Archives

This photo of the John Green Store is in the early 1930s after Alameda County forced the removal of the porch because of the widened roadway. There is at this time a stucco exterior. The Dublin Library is in the left portion of the building. DHPA Photo

This is the Green Store in 1988. The structure, with its porch rebuilt and restored by the Dublin Historical Preservation Association, is a registered landmark. Author Photo

Stockton or Dublin Road soon became the Lincoln Highway across the valley. Here in the 1920s a Dublin service station serves the public. It was located across the road from Hansen's Garage. ALVHS Archives

The Amador Garage was operated by Eriksen and Nielsen and stood on the north side of Dublin Boulevard next to Dougherty's Station. Among other products, associated gasoline and genuine parts for Chevrolets and Oaklands were sold. DHPA Photo

In 1914, the Dublin Garage provided services to automobiles and motorcycles. Note the sign "Vulcanizing," a welcome sight to motorists with the unreliable tires of the time. The garage was located on the south side of Dublin Boulevard next to the Dublin Hotel. DHPA Photo

In the foreground of this photo is the Dublin Garage and the Dublin Hotel. A drive through the old crossroads today reveals most of the trees of bygone days have disappeared. DHPA Photo

By the late 1870s Dublin had two hotels, a general store, harness and shoe shops, and a blacksmith. Shown here is the Amador Valley Hotel (also known as the Dublin Hotel), which was operated by the Reimers family at that time. DHPA Photo

This is the Dublin Hotel as it looked with an addition and signs in the 1930s. The crossroads where early Dublin or Dougherty's Station businesses were located can be identified today as Dublin Boulevard and Donlon Way. ALVHS Archives

BOERO'S

DUBLIN HOTEL

Restaurant — Bar — Cocktail Lounge

Favorite Cowboy Rendezvous

Of course, we would all like to go to the Dublin Hotel at 1932 prices. Here reproduced is a well-worn, spotted menu from the hotel at the time it was run by the Boero family during the Depression years. Moller family Photo

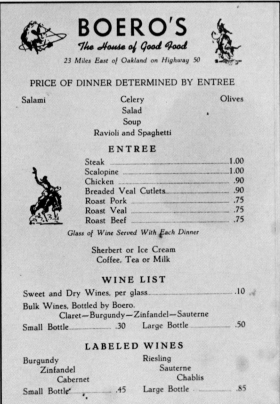

BOERO'S
The House of Good Food
23 Miles East of Oakland on Highway 50

PRICE OF DINNER DETERMINED BY ENTREE

Salami	Celery	Olives
	Salad	
	Soup	
	Ravioli and Spaghetti	

ENTREE

Steak	1.00
Scalopine	1.00
Chicken	.90
Breaded Veal Cutlets	.90
Roast Pork	.75
Roast Veal	.75
Roast Beef	.75

Glass of Wine Served With Each Dinner

Sherbert or Ice Cream
Coffee, Tea or Milk

WINE LIST

Sweet and Dry Wines, per glass .... .10
Bulk Wines, Bottled by Boero
Claret—Burgundy—Zinfandel—Sauterne
Small Bottle ...... .30   Large Bottle ...... .50

LABELED WINES

Burgundy	Riesling
Zinfandel	Sauterne
Cabernet	Chablis

Small Bottle ...... .45   Large Bottle ...... .85

SANDWICHES

Roast Pork	.15	Salami	.15
Roast Beef	.15	Liverwurst	.15
Roast Veal	.15	Tuna	.20
Boiled Ham	.15	Sardine (Imported)	.20
Fried Ham	.20	Hot Roast Pork	.25
Fried Egg	.15	Hot Roast Beef	.25
Cheese (Domestic)	.15	Hot Roast Veal	.25
Cheese (Imported)	.20	Fried Ham and Egg	.25
Tomato and Lettuce	.15	Ham and Cheese	.25

SALADS

Crab	.35	Potato	.20
Combination	.25	Sliced Tomato	.25

A LA CARTE

STEAKS			
		Scalopine	.60
T-Bone	1.00	Breaded Veal Cutlets	.60
Extra Cut T-Bone	1.50	Half Chicken	.60
Rib Steak	.75	Home Made Ravioli	.35
Extra Cut Rib Steak	1.00	Spaghetti	.25
New York Cut	.60	Half and Half	.30
Extra Cut New York Cut	.75	Cold Plate	.50

EGGS AND OMELETTES

Ham and Eggs	.45
Bacon and Eggs	.45
Plain Omelette	.30
Ham Omelette	.40
Two Eggs (any style)	.25

Not Responsible for Lost Articles

No Order Under 10c at Tables

Visit Our BAR and COCKTAIL LOUNGE

Livermore

When the new town of Livermore was beginning to prosper, a hub of the community called Mill Square developed at the east end of First Street. It is depicted here in about 1869 in a drawing from Thompson and West. ALVHS Archives

Central Pacific (later Southern Pacific) Railroad depots looked much the same in all communities. Pictured here is a train arriving in Livermore about 1910. In modern times the depot was restored by the Livermore Heritage Guild and now houses offices. Dopking Photo

In 1910 the first Western Pacific Railroad train came through the town of Pleasanton. In this old, deteriorated print it appears as if most of the tiny community turned out for the event. *John Edmands Collection, ALVHS Archives*

Up and down the Western Pacific Railroad line the stations took on the same look, the mission influence architectural style. *Dopking Photo*

This 1950s photo of a freight train passing through Altamont portrays the architectural style of the Central Pacific (Southern Pacific) Railroad stations. *LHG Archives*

The station in Sunol, unlike those in Pleasanton, Livermore, Altamont, and so many others, is only a one story structure. Here in 1908 a freight train moves through. Central Pacific built all the stations and then sold out to Southern Pacific. Day Collection Photo, ALVHS Archives

In 1924 the first Burlington passenger train came through Pleasanton. Shown here at the Pleasanton Western Pacific Depot, it is greeted by a group of townspeople, including J. H. Stahlnecker, station agent. The boast at the time was only seventy-two hours from San Francisco to Chicago. This train was the forerunner of the famous California Zephyr with its all silver domed cars. Photo courtesy of E. H. "Herb" Stahlnecker

From the late 1880s until the turn of the century, Livermore grew quickly as the center of commerce in the Amador-Livermore Valley. Along with that growth came newspapers, such as the Echo, *established in 1882 as a monthly publication for three years and then as a weekly until 1919.*

William Still was editor with his son Elmer as helper. A humorous anecdote of the time was that Still rode around on a bicycle and children of the town teased him with, "Keep still and you'll hear the echo."

Other newspapers included the Star *established in 1883, which became the* Pleasanton Times *in 1885 and in 1971* The Valley Times. *In Sunol, the* Sentinel *began publishing in the 1880s. In 1874 the* Livermore Enterprise *began publishing, and became the* Livermore Herald *in 1876. The* Herald *merged with the* Livermore News *and became the* Herald and News *in 1956. It is now the* Tri-Valley Herald. *Sarboraria Photo*

In 1875 A. J. McLeod plotted the second addition to the original town of Livermore, an oddly shaped area to the east of First Street named the McLeod Tract. In 1888 he constructed the building shown here, fittingly known as the McLeod Building. Over the years it has housed two banks, a dentist's office, the Masonic Lodge (third floor), and several businesses. It was considered in the late 1880s to be the elite building of the time. ALVHS Archives

Life wasn't always easy in downtown Livermore. This is an example of high water in 1907 and 1911 when the Arroyo Mocho overflowed out by Concannon Winery and sent water all the way down Lizzie Street and beyond.

Here in front of the McLeod Building a horse, a buggy, and passengers pose as the water flows by while onlookers stand dry on the permanent covered sidewalk. Sarboraria Photo

At the corner of First and Lizzie Streets workmen sandbag the entryway to the bank and the Herald office during the highwater. Sarboraria Photo

In the 1930s, as in other years, the Arroyo Mocho ran full during heavy winter and spring rains. Here a brave motorist risks all as he attempts a crossing on Holmes Street (Vallecitos Road). In the background (very dark) is Charlie Ginger's house. He was an old Indian fighter who claimed to have been scalped. Sarboraria Photo

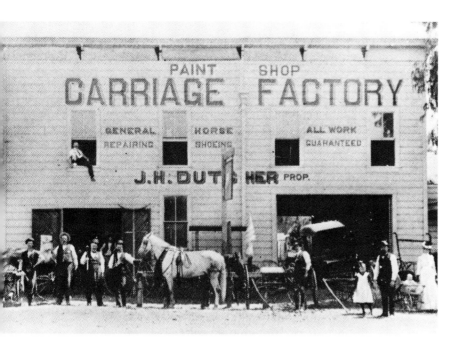

In 1890 the Jay H. Dutcher Carriage Factory was located on Second Street in Livermore. The Livermore Bank is now on that site. Dutcher's daughter, Vera Crane, incidentally, was a sixth grade teacher who very strictly gave every student that traditional English language (grammar) foundation. LHG Archives

In the 1880s the Ryan Brothers Livery Stable was operating on Lizzie Street (Livermore Avenue). The draying business hauled supplies to the coal mines at Tesla, east of Livermore. ALVHS Archives

The N. D. Dutcher hardware store was operating in Livermore in 1880. In 1882 a second half was built, doubling the store size. ALVHS Archives

Interior of the Dutcher hardware store at the turn of the century shows (left to right) owner N. D. Dutcher, Sr.; N. D. Dutcher, Jr.; Dan Luce; and John J. Jensen, Sr. LHG Archives

In the 1880s it was common for women to gather for fittings and dressmaking. Here is Miss M. Grath's dressmaking parlor in Livermore. ALVHS Archives

This photo of the Farmers Exchange Hotel on L Street at the railroad tracks in Livermore was probably taken in the 1880s. The building later served as the

Greyhound Bus Depot for many years and was demolished in 1968 to make way for a Colonel Sanders Restaurant franchise. ALVHS Archives

Built in the 1870s, the Washington Hotel at First and L streets, Livermore, underwent several renovations and name changes. The Mally family owners renamed it Mally's Hotel (the Annex) about 1910 and later in 1930 called it the Palace Hotel. ALVHS Archives

The Masons left the McLeod Building in 1908 after the completion of the Masonic Building on the corner of Livermore Avenue and First Street. Housed there were a bank, pool hall, a dentist's office, and other businesses. Dopking Photo

The automobile had not arrived, and the streets were not yet paved. Pictured here about 1890 is First Street in Livermore looking west toward Pleasanton five miles away. The mud of a rainy winter and the dust of hot, dry summers would remain before First Street was designated a state highway and paving authorized in 1914. Sarboraria Photo

This is an east-facing view of First Street in 1900-1910. ALVHS Archives

This is a closeup of the north side of First Street at J Street showing the Post Office around 1910. Sarboraria Photo

Carlo Ferrario's Livermore Saloon in 1910-1915 located at Second and L Streets. It remains open for business today as Gardella's Liquor Store. *Dopking Photo*

This interior scene is typical of the saloons operating at the turn of the century. In about 1915 the Hub was a popular spot at the east end of First Street. Lizzie's Fountain is now located there. *Sarboraria Photo*

Frank Beigbedier owned and operated the Livermore French Laundry in 1910. Located on Second Street, the business at last report continues to operate today. *Dopking Photo*

At the turn of the century, electricity had arrived in the Amador-Livermore Valley but not refrigeration. The California Meat Market in Livermore about 1910 had to rely on ice storage for slaughtered animals. The Stoeven name now operates a large meat packing plant near Dixon, California. Dopking Photo

Interior of the California Meat Market. Dopking Photo

In 1906 business calendars were quite elaborate. This one from the W. R. Stoeven California Market in Livermore was multi-colored and about thirty inches high with individual tear-off pages for the months. Moller Family Photo

Billy Wilson's California Transfer Company around 1915 moves a load of power poles for continuing valley electrification away from the Central Pacific (Southern Pacific) Depot in Livermore. Dopking Photo

The Diamond Flour Mill was located on the north side of First Street in 1915. R. A. Hansen was the last owner. Before that the mill belonged to C. J. Stevens and was located elsewhere in Livermore. It was then moved to the First Street site. LHG Photo

Theodore Gorner had a furniture store in 1900. This interior may well show him standing by the pile of folded floor coverings. ALVHS Archives

From 1910-1930 the George Beck grocery store operated in Livermore on First Street. Interestingly, several sizes of hemp rope were also on sale, as can be seen in front of the counter coming up through holes in the floor. The large coils of rope were obviously stored in the basement. ALVHS Archives

Livermore Commercial Company is another example of a grocery store operating around 1915 in that city. LHG Archives

By 1915 the automobile was beginning to make an appearance, and the livery stables and harness shops were slowly giving way to maintenance and repair shops. Here is the interior of Crane's Livermore Garage where they also sold Model T Fords. LHG Archives

At Second and J streets in Livermore the Bell Theatre operated showing the latest motion pictures. It burned about 1910 and the theatre moved to First Street into the new Schenone Building. LHG Archives

The Schenone Building on First Street a few doors away from the site of the well-known Livermore flagpole had a saloon. Some changes have been made in the lower floor over the years, but a "watering hole" continues to do business. The Independent newspaper has occupied the second floor since 1963. Dopking Photo

It is easily seen that the Schenone Building and those around it have undergone great commercial change from the turn of the century to the 1930s. The Bell Theatre became the State and a cafe and a soda shop and a drug store opened around it. Croce's in the 1920s was a favorite place for politicians and bootleggers. The cafe eventually moved to Lodi, California, where it still operates. ALVHS Archives

Darrow's Bakery, Ice Cream, and Coffee Parlor in Livermore operated on First Street near K Street in the 1920s. Note that the business, called The Arrow, also advertises fine candies. On the front of the store are two signs advertising chewing tobacco, Star and Climax Plug. Sarboraria Photo

As America's love affair with the automobile grew, many primitive dealerships, repair shops, and service stations opened. Here in the early 1920s the F. H. Duarte Highway Garage advertises Star and Durant automobiles (no longer manufactured). This business was located on the Lincoln Highway, also known as Dublin Road, Stockton Road, Old Highway, and now as Junction Avenue. ALVHS Archives

Later in the 1920s and into the 1930s the true service station emerged. Here the Livermore Service Station at First and L streets shows specialization in selling gasoline and oil and offering to wash the windshield, check air in the tires, and look under the hood for oil, water, and battery fluid levels. Those days seem to be gone forever. Sarboraria Photo

Pleasanton

From the middle of Main Street, Pleasanton, around 1900, across from the Johnston Building at Rose Avenue looking south, there isn't much to see but smooth, unpaved gravel roadway and a few structures. On the right is what is now the Starting Gate bar, and next door was the Mavis Pavilion, since burned, but for years the location for theatrical companies to perform, balls and parties to be held, and other celebrations. Records show that owner Joseph Nevis was also proprieter of the Bohemian Cafe next door to the pavilion, probably today's bar. Dopking Photo

Looking north on Main Street, the first very recognizable structure is the "White Corner," or today known as Kolln Hardware. In 1869 C. A. Wise opened a tinshop at the corner of Main and Division streets. In 1890 the hardware store was constructed and Wise sold out to Frank and Bert Lewis. Then in 1905 James Cruikshank and H. G. Kolln took over the Lewis Brothers operation. In 1933 Kolln became sole owner. ALVHS Archives

The interior of the Kolln Tinsmith and Plumbing Shop at Main and Division in 1906 shows (left to right) Herman Kolln, Chester Abrott, and Peter Bruess. The fourth person was not identified. ALVHS Archives

The immediately recognizable Main Street landmark building is seen here in 1915 after Cruikshank and Kolln took over the business. Their stock offered a variety of hardware, furniture, plumbing supplies, household items, and other merchandizable wares of the times. ALVHS Archives

The Philip H. Kolb general merchandise building was constructed in 1890 and is seen here in 1902 decked out in patriotic flags and bunting, probably in celebration of the Fourth of July. Kolb owned several parcels on Main Street, as well as warehouse and rural properties where he raised sugar beets, cattle, horses, and swine. ALVHS Archives

The Fashion Livery and Sale Stable was in business at Main and Division (between Kolln Hardware and the Rose Hotel) from the early 1890s through the turn of the century. Owners were A. F. Schweer and Lee Wells. The business was typical of livery stables of the times but added a dimension, the sale of horses due to the interest in the Pleasanton track. ALVHS Archives

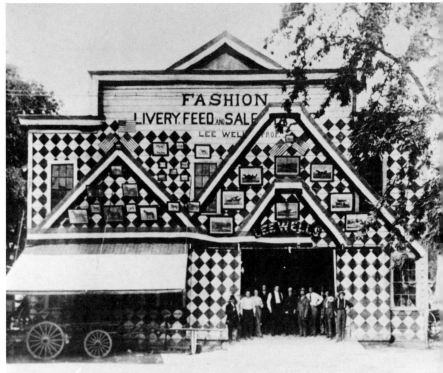

A Mr. C. Letham arrived in Pleasanton in 1898 and proceeded to buy out the Haggerty Bakery on Main Street. By 1901 he was in business and supplying the hotels and local families with bread, pies, cakes, and other pastries. Shown here is the place of business and the delivery wagon for his Letham's Home Bakery. *ALVHS Archives*

The (George) Johnston Building was completed in 1896 and is shown here between 1900 and 1905 with a permanent awning over the sidewalk (now gone). Other businesses at the time were a harness shop and a candy shop. In the last eighty years or so among the businesses in the building were a restaurant, a shoe store, an office supply store, an art gallery, and now antiques and another firm upstairs. The Pleasanton street location in 1900 was Main and Neal. Today it is Main and Rose. *ALVHS Archives*

At the turn of the century the old Bank of Pleasanton was located in this brick building on Neal Street next to the Southern Pacific Depot. The building also housed a meat market. In modern times, law offices and the justice court have used the space, as well as a private residence on the second floor.

Not many crossing signs are around any more. Children today have probably not heard the riddle: "Railroad crossing, look out for the cars. Can you spell it without any R's?" *ALVHS Archives, Dopking Photo*

John Kottinger built the original Farmers Hotel in 1864. It burned in 1898 but was immediately rebuilt by H. Reimers. The hostelry boasted electricity, fourteen rooms, a dining room, and a bar. The structure is located on the west side at the north end of Main Street alongside the Arroyo Del Valle. The modern business is now operated as the Pleasanton Hotel with bar and dining room but offices occupy its rooms upstairs. ALVHS Archives

The Rose Hotel was located on the east side of Main Street between Division and Neal. As pictured here in 1902, it boasted a total of thirty rooms, a dining room, a bar, and entertainment. It was the meeting place for all interested in thoroughbred horses and in racing. The building was demolished in the 1950s and the Amador Valley Savings and Loan bank building and parking lot takes its place. ALVHS Archives

The original Pleasanton Hotel, now the site of a service station, located on the northwest corner of Main and St. Mary streets, is shown here as it looked at the turn of the century. It was built in 1868 by John Kottinger and sold to Herman Detjens who came from San Francisco to run it. The first Masonic Lodge was formed here in 1871, now Mosaic Lodge 219 in Livermore. The hotel burned in 1915 and was not rebuilt. ALVHS Archives

The Lamothe Pleasanton French Laundry operated in the 1920s and before. Here the delivery wagon is still horse-drawn. ALVHS Archives

The old Bank of PLeasanton became the Bank of America (Bank of Italy) at the corner of Main and Neal streets in the Arendt Building. The telephone operator and exchange and the post office were also there at the time. When Bank of America moved to a new location, the building was converted to general merchandise business use. On the site originally was a business which sold farm equipment and hardware, first the Wallace Company and then Arendt. *Dopking Photo*

First National Bank of Pleasanton and Amador Valley Savings Bank opened for business in 1910. (They merged in 1938.) The building shown here at Main and Spring streets was completed in 1911 and the bank moved in. It remained there until 1968 when the bank moved to larger quarters at Main and St. John streets. In 1980 the bank chose a new name, Community First National Bank. *First National Bank Photo*

For years Pleasanton was a rose growing center, and First National Bank celebrated with an annual community Mother's Day Rose Show in the bank lobby. Beginning in 1938, the show soon grew in size to cover all available area in the bank, both in front and behind teller cages. Shown here is the narrow old building with an early show in the late 1930s or early 1940s. *First National Bank Photo*

Completed in 1896, 450 Main Sreet was one of the first brick buildings and had a merchantile store from that time to around 1920 on the southeast corner of Main and Neal streets. The Arendt and Company was in business there selling work and dress clothing and shoes. ALVHS Archives

This picture was taken around 1960 and represents B. H. "Boo" Hall's hay, grain, general livestock feed, and paint store at 450 Main Street. In the early 1900s the E. E. Hall warehouses were located at First and Abbie streets for hay and grain storage, the sale of farm implements, the operation of a barley mill, and also the sale of lumber, cement, wool, rope and wire, and burlap. ALVHS Archives

In the 1930s this service station at the corner of Main and St. Mary streets was operated by John J. Amaral. It continues in operation today but with modern pumps. Not much else has changed except that the lubrication rack in the building at the rear is no longer there. This is the site of the original Pleasanton Hotel that was destroyed by fire in 1915. *ALVHS Archives*

From 1867 through 1963 the Mary Rose Guanziroli family had businesses in Pleasanton. Pictured here in the 1920s at the south end of Main Street (122 just before the Southern Pacific tracks) is the old Associated service station, long since demolished. This photo taken by grandson Bill Azevedo. *ALVHS Archives*

In the 1930s and into the 1950s Jim's Creamery operated in its central location on the east side of Main Street. Pictured (left to right) are owner Anton Georgis, customer Betty Arendt, Jim Georgis, and customer Marguerite Passeggi. ALVHS Archives

In 1936 Pleasanton had its own movie theatre at 641 Main Street (west side). The building in later years housed a large family clothing store and now sales of antique furniture. The old theatre was built by Charles Chicazolla, former owner of the Lincoln Theatre at 511 Main (no longer standing). ALVHS Archives

Sunol

It is said that Sunol (five miles south of Pleasanton at the head of Niles Canyon), in the late 1800s, was a busy bustling small community with a number of businesses, a church, a school, and two hotels.

James Trimingham moved to the Sunol area in 1866 and farmed. In 1880 the family moved to the center of town. Pictured here at the turn of the century is the Trimingham Store which sold general merchandise, feed, and hay.

James W. Trimingham, son of John (one of eight children), now resides on Second Street in Pleasanton. ALVHS Archives

The two photos of the nearby Hazel Glen Hotel about 1900 are from the Arthur Day collection. He owned a livery stable in Sunol. The hotel burned in 1910. ALVHS Archives

Three days before Christmas in 1987 a landmark on Sunol's main street, the historic Lyon's Brewery which dates back to 1862, was destroyed by fire. Three other businesses also burned, which amounted to about half of the commercial business there. Plans are underway to rebuild. Pictured here from the rear view is tragic evidence of the devastation. Author Photo

Owner Frank Louthan put up his new sign seven or eight years ago. Julie Banta made it much like the historic original. The business previously had been the Temple Bar. Sunolian Photo

Sunol Hay and Feed burned along with the brewery, as did an adjacent insurance office. Sunolian Photo

*This September harvest scene is before
the turn of the century and probably in
the Cresta Blanca Vineyards near Livermore. LHG Archives*

Chapter 3

Grain, Hops, Sugar Beets, Cattle, Horses, and Wine

It is known that as early as 1856 Robert Livermore was growing wheat and barley and was cutting wild oat hay. He also raised cattle, horses, and sheep. By the 1870s grain and hay dominated the agriculture of the valley and this remained true until the 1950s. From the 1930s through the 1960s with good irrigation the valley was able to support rose hybridization (Jackson and Perkins Company) and hundreds of acres of commercial tomato growing.

Before the gasoline-powered tractor, harvest crews used stationary threshing machines powered by steam engines. The operation even had a chuck wagon with a cook who came along.

In the 1880s hops, sugar, beets, and berries were grown in what was termed the "swampy seasonal lake" west and north of Pleasanton. By 1900 these were the largest hop fields in California with much of the crop going to London, England, for ale brewing although a brewery did exist in Livermore in 1874.

By the 1880s rail cars left the valley loaded with coal, livestock, grain, hay, hops, fruits, vegetables, olives, nuts, sand, glass, brick and potter's clay, wine, sugar beets, and more.

Today most of the farm land has given way to suburban home and shopping center development. One large agricultural influence remains, that of the vineyards and winemaking.

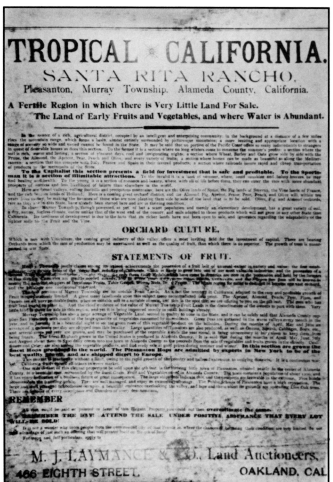

From the 1870s through the turn of the century, Livermore was not the only place undergoing subdividing. It was happening to the farm land even then in Pleasanton. In 1894 north of town the Oakland Land and Improvement Company set up an auction of land parcels in an area we would now identify as northeast from about Black Avenue to the Freeway.

A large poster or handbill proclaimed the Santa Rita Rancho as fertile land for fruits and vegetables where water is abundant. The headline proclaimed "Tropical California" and especially invited "capitalists" to invest. Courtesy of Donna Kamp McMillion

On the back side of the handbill was a subdivided map showing lots and larger parcels to be sold at auction. What we now call Black Avenue to the east of Santa Rita Road was then named Pleasanton Avenue. No such through road exists today, a school being situated there. Not connected but aligned with Valley Avenue was a street or road called Santa Rita Avenue. Up at the corner of Dublin-Livermore Road was another group of small parcels. It is difficult to tell whether the map was drawn to scale and whether these alignments are entirely correct. Courtesy of Donna Kamp McMillion

In 1898 Henry Mohr had as many as three steam engines such as these operating in his grain harvest. This photo is of a horse-drawn machine, but he also owned one which could propel itself from location to location where it would be set up at the end of a long belt and fed straw to make steam power to run the thresher. Mohr's property was north and east between Pleasanton and Livermore. ALVHS Archives

Henry Mohr stands by one of his tractors, this one able to move from place to place, be set up, and provide power to run a thresher or other machinery. ALVHS Archives

A model similar to Mohr's steam tractor is seen here in the 1987 Alameda County Fair Parade. A large display of antique farm machinery is displayed annually at the fair in Pleasanton and continues throughout the year on loan to valley schools. Curator Bob Graham will pre-arrange tours of the machinery at the fairgrounds. *ALVHS Archives*

Maas Luders cultivated several hundred acres west of Livermore near where the airport is now located. In 1878 he had a steam engine similar to that of Henry Mohr. It was a model made by the Rice Company of Hayward with the boiler built in San Francisco. This machine is now at the University of California at Davis Agriculture Museum. August Hagemann is pictured here standing on a plow pulled by a 1915 Case gasoline-powered tractor, the first in the valley. *ALVHS Archives*

62

August Hagemann bought his Case tractor at the Panama-Pacific Exposition in San Francisco in 1915. Here on the Hagemann ranch near Livermore is the tractor with the traditional long belt to the machinery. The threat of fire kept the old steam engine power source a long way from the thresher. The new tractor slowly changed that. ALVHS Archives

Around the turn of the century, several thousand train carloads of bailed hay were shipped annually from the Amador-Livermore Valley. Pictured here, probably in 1920 or before, is Johnny Johnson's hay press working in a field near Oak Knoll Cemetery west of Livermore. ALVHS Archives

Not all of the wheat and barley threshing was done out in the middle of a field. Here the machinery has been parked close to the barn so the chaff can be deposited directly into the barn loft, saving many man hours of hauling and pitchforking hay by hand. Dopking Photo

By the 1940s, the barley harvest had become mobile with gasoline and diesel track-laying tractors pulling harvesters able to move about the field to cut, thresh, and sack the harvest. Dopking Photo

At the turn of the century, F. W. Brenzel was using this machine to drill water wells in the valley. He is said to have been the most prestigious driller in the valley. ALVHS Archives

A similar well drilling machine shown here has brought in an artesian well. Wells were of extreme importance in the dry summer months for irrigation, livestock, and everyday supplies to the farmhouse. Without a pump, only the best wells would run the year around. Artesian wells were found to the west of Pleasanton, but not near Livermore. Sarboraria Photo

Sugar Beets

Sugar beet farming began in the valley in the 1800s and continued as a strong crop well into the 1950s. At the turn of the century, as many as two hundred workers were employed with as many as a thousand rail cars or more being shipped to a processing plant in the south bay (Alvarado). The location of the pictured field is near Mohr Avenue north of Pleasanton. The harvesters are of the 1940-1950 vintage, the crop being grown by Mel Nielsen. ALVHS Archives

In the 1890s, wagons loaded with sacks of sugar beets lined up in Pleasanton to be loaded onto rail cars. The pickers and loaders have hitched a ride to town aboard the wagons after a long day in the fields. DHPA Photo

As early as 1885, experiments in hop growing were taking place in the valley. Soon after, most of a nineteen hundred acre portion of the Rancho del Valle to the north and west of Pleasanton was planted, making it the largest growing area for hops in California. The swampy region was especially well-suited for this type of crop.

About the first of September as many as fifteen hundred persons would be employed to pick hops. Pictured here about 1900 is the local Casterson family, all in the harvest. *ALVHS Archives*

Pleasanton Hop Company pickers would bring their hoppers to the end of a row for weighing and tallying. The fields began about a half mile west of Pleasanton and rows extended for more than a mile. Vines grew from wires on top twenty-foot poles and strings to the ground to climb on. Free-flowing artesian wells provided irrigation water during the dry summer. *ALVHS Archives*

From the Kolln family album of the 1880s is this picture of a huge hop kiln dryer west of Pleasanton. Green hops were heated with forced sulphur air to sterilize them and remove moisture. They were pressed into large bales and stored in warehouses until time for shipment. *ALVHS Archives*

A dozen large hop kilns were used to dry the harvest. Much of the finished product went for a time to the Guinness Brewery, London, England. Storage warehouses are seen in the center of this picture, taken about 1900. ALVHS Archives

In this late 1800s picture from the Kolln family album, hundreds of workers from as far away as the San Joaquin Valley have come with their own tents to live and work in the hop harvest. Grocery, butcher, and bakery wagons came to the camp from Pleasanton to sell supplies. The company provided artesian water and sanitary services. Workers who did not wish to prepare their own food used a restaurant at the camp. ALVHS Archives

The final step in hop processing was shipment. Here at the turn of the century are wagons at the Southern Pacific Depot in Pleasanton ready to unload bales of pressed, dry hops. Some were shipped as far away as Australia. ALVHS Archives

The following five pictures show several scenes from a variety of farming and animal raising pursuits. All are from a collection belonging to Dagmar Orloff Fulton family and were taken in the 1920s and early 1930s.

Hay is moved by hand for storage in the barn.

This is the mobile grain elevator and seed cleaner.

The tractor generates electricity for light in order to lengthen the long work day.

69

A sheep shearing demonstration instructs local citizens.

Even with large dray animals being replaced by the tractor, the horseshoer remains in demand for race horses. Photos courtesy of Dagmar Orloff Fulton

As hop growing began to decline in the early 1900s, dairying emerged in the valley. Names from the 1950s include Koopmann, Friesman, Hansen, Orloff, Holdener, and the Fox and Meadowlark Dairies. Pictured here are different views of the Hansen-Orloff Dairy number two, which was located on the south side of Hopyard Road a half mile from Pleasanton.

Dairy number one was located west of Santa Rita Road on Black Avenue, generally in the area behind Amador Valley High School. It was the site chosen for a college campus, but politics intervened and now the California State University is at Hayward. The Orloff family sold out and the dairy closed in 1964, the land soon to be filled with homes.

The dairy had split in 1947 with the Hopyard Road portion going to Hans N. Hansen and the Black Avenue location to Thomas J. Orloff. The original dairy began in 1919. Following the close of the Orloff half, Hansen decided to sell out several years later. His land, too, now contains homes.

In both photos hop kilns and warehouses remain. The dairy used these old buildings for storage of hay, feed, and equipment and built milking barns. Photos courtesy of Dagmar Orloff Fulton

These are typical dairy barns of the 1920s. Above is a classic hay and feed barn with the high peaked roof to allow for bringing hay into the loft.

The second is a low roof style used for milking. Also seen in the foreground is the inevitable by-product of animals, manure, and horse-drawn spreader. *Photos courtesy of Dagmar Orloff Fulton*

Even though Robert Livermore planted a vineyard (home use) in the mid 1840s and John Kottinger (first commercial) near Pleasanton in 1850, the boom in grape growing and winemaking didn't occur in the Amador-Livermore Valley until the mid to late 1880s. The success lasted only about thirty years because in 1918 laws were being entered on the books to restrict alcoholic beverage sales, and by 1920 it was all over—Prohibition!

In the following pages an attempt has been made to illustrate early winemaking in the valley. With so many vineyards and wineries operating, it is impossible here to include all of them. A good place to start reading

for those interested is in Janet Newton's soft-cover booklet titled *Stories of the Vineyards and Wineries of the Livermore Valley.*

Two immigrants arrived in 1883 to plant vines on Tesla Road. Carl Wente came from Germany and James Concannon from Ireland. According to some, the Ruby Hill vineyard was also begun in 1883, the property of John Crellin. It later became Stony Ridge Winery, which is still operating but not in the original buildings. It is run by the Scotto Family of Pleasanton. The property is presently owned by Wente Brothers Winery.

The Carl H. Wente family and winery workers pose sometime before the 1906 earthquake. The water tank tower, in this picture, is still standing. It was destroyed in the earthquake of 1906. ALVHS Archives

James and Ellen Concannon are shown here with their children in 1895. ALVHS Archives

Carl F. Wente and wife Barbara pose with their young family in 1894. ALVHS Archives

Through the years Louis Mel kept his interest in viticulture. He is shown here celebrating (and posing) on his ninety-eighth birthday, September 23, 1936. *ALVHS Archives*

Louis Mel, seen here in 1896, was typical of the vineyard planters and wine-makers of the mid 1800s. He and his wife arrived in the valley in 1884, bought property on Vineyard Avenue (Tesla Road), planted forty acres in vines, and opened a winery. They retired in 1916, selling their property and moving to Oakland. *ALVHS Archives*

Another of the very early wineries was the Olivina Estate, vineyards established about 1882. Julius Paul Smith and wife Sarah had two thousand acres of grapes, olives, and walnuts. He died in 1904, and Sarah stopped wine production in 1908. *ALVHS Archives*

Both Howard and Joseph Black had vineyards in 1887. Shown here about 1900 is a group of pickers and grape haulers in the Black Ranch Vineyard. Nick Livermore is the driver. *ALVHS Archives*

About three miles east of Pleasanton Lou Crellin had a tract of 450 acres, most of which had been planted in vineyard in 1883, making it one of the earliest. The Ruby Hill Winery was in the three-story brick building seen here. A distillery for brandy was next to the main structure. Capacity of the winery is said to have been 300,000 gallons. In modern times this winery, although under several owners, was and is known as Stony Ridge. ALVHS Archives

Many winery buildings were constructed on a hillside in order to take advantage of gravity flow at the time of crush. Here in 1897 at the rear or up side (second level) of the Ruby Hill Winery grapes are being weighed in and dumped into the crusher. Crushers here were operated by steam power and the wine presses by hydraulic pressure. ALVHS Archives

A white chalk cliff south of Livermore inspired Charles Wetmore to name his vineyard and winery Cresta Blanca, another early winemaking business in 1882. He championed California wines here and also in France at the Paris Exposition. On a second trip to France he procured cuttings of several varieties to graft to his vines in California. In 1889 Cresta Blanca wine won the Grand Prize at the Paris Exhibition.

Pictured here are the caves into the chalk cliffs which were used for wine storage. Today Wente Brothers, new owners, have made them into champagne cellars. LHG Archives

Shown here are two scenes in the Cresta Blanca bottling room around the turn of the century. LHG Archives

The only information on this photo is "crushing grapes near Livermore." Shown is a hand-operated basket press at the left and a hand-operated pump at the right. LHG Archives

On the upper level boxes of grapes are being dumped into the crusher. Below large presses are receiving the juice and must. Both photos were probably taken at the Cresta Blanca Winery in the 1890s. ALVHS Archives

The Mont Rouge Winery was located on the west edge of Livermore near the old Oak Knoll Cemetery (near Granada High School). Wine was being produced in 1887 and in 1889 owner and native of France A. G. Chauche won a gold medal at the Paris Exposition. The business did not survive Prohibition, and the building burned in the early 1930s. Sarboraria Photo

Charles and Peter Raboli, natives of Italy, built this winery building at Second and K streets, Livermore, in 1910. Today it has a coat of stucco and houses another business. The Rabolis had a vineyard but purchased grapes from other growers. Sarboraria Photo

Using "Fresno Scrapers," workmen dig a cellar for Carlo Ferrario Winery on Second Street in Livermore. The time is probably the early 1900s. Charlie Gardella is in the center holding a scraper. This location is now the Wells Fargo Bank parking lot. Sarboraria Photo

Prohibition closed all of the wineries from 1920 until 1932 except for the Concannon Vineyards. Sacramental wines for church services were vinted, but the trade in commercial wines ended here, as everywhere else. This view is through the vineyard at the rear of the winery. LHG Archives

This old carriage house near Sunol was built by Thomas F. Batchelder in 1887. It, too, housed a winery in the heyday of winemaking in the Amador-Livermore Valley. ALVHS Archives

Wineries in the Amador-Livermore
Valley operating in 1988 include
Concannon, Elliston, Fenestra, Liver-
more Valley Cellars, Retzlaff, Stony
Ridge, and Wente. Pictured is a side
view of the main house restoration
adjacent to the winery building at
Elliston on Kilkare Road in Sunol.
Sunolian Photo

Stony Ridge Winery recently moved the
old Villa Armando tasting room from
St. John Street in Pleasanton to Tesla
Road east of Livermore (between
Concannon and Wente). The new
home (tasting room and visitor center)
is planned to be open the summer of
1988. Author Photo

Built in 1886, the Dr. Gordon home at Fourth and K streets in Livermore was moved out on Tesla Road near the Concannon Winery for restoration. It is an example of one of the larger mansion-type structures of the time. ALVHS Archives

Chapter 4

Adobes, Homes, Houses, and Buildings

Not many examples remain of the earliest structures built in the Amador-Livermore Valley. A few have been preserved and given heritage status. The communities of Pleasanton, Livermore, Dublin, and Sunol have examples of some of the finest old homes, most built from about 1880 through 1920.

A sampling of those old homes and buildings is presented in the pages that follow. A drive through the residential sections of either Pleasanton or Livermore reveals many more. The Amador-Livermore Valley Historical Society on Main Street in Pleasanton, the Livermore Heritage Guild in the Carnegie Building in Livermore, and the Dublin Historical Preservation Association have additional photos and information.

John Kottinger built this frame house in 1851 near the surviving adobe barn on Ray Street, Pleasanton. It was torn down around 1930. ALVHS Archives

The Kottinger adobe barn was built in 1851, and when John Kottinger became an Alameda County judge, it was used as a jail. This picture was probably taken in the 1930s. ALVHS Archives

Today the Kottinger barn houses an antique business. The structure was renovated with complete interior support by Robert Koopmann of Pleasanton. It is now a registered historical landmark. Author Photo

The Francisco Solano Alviso adobe, located west of Pleasanton on Foothill Road, once served as headquarters for John C. Fremont during the Mexican War in California. The conflict ended in 1848. In modern times this structure and several other outbuildings served as the Meadowlark Dairy. ALVHS Archives, Don Lane Photo

Now abandoned, the buildings face extinction. Plans are underway to demolish some to make way for home construction. The adobe, however, has been designated as a historical site. Shown here is the entrance today adjacent to Foothill Road, a view of the rear, left side of the main building. In the photo above the structure faces east. Author Photo

The Robert Livermore home here pictured was his second, the first was an adobe and is no longer standing. Two separate buildings make up this structure, the two-story in the rear being a pre-fabricated addition built in 1850. The lower front portion was the kitchen. Chester Anderson owned the property when this picture was taken in the 1930s. This building also is no longer standing. Sarboraria photo

Maas Luders stands by the side entrance gate to his home, which he built in 1883, west of Livermore. He had come to the valley in 1862 and married Maria Hagemann. Maas bragged that this house contained eight thousand bricks and cost him a total of $8,000 to build. He was known as one of the leading grain farmers in the valley, at one time farming much of the land between Livermore and Pleasanton. Standing on the gate and leaning on the post is Herbert L. Hagemann, Sr. ALVHS Archives

This front view photo of the Luders home was taken in 1965. It was burned by the Livermore Fire Department as a training exercise. The land is now a part of the Livermore Airport. ALVHS Archives

Another successful farmer in the valley was Henry P. Mohr. Cornelius Mohr (Henry's father) bought this home north of Pleasanton in 1885 from John English. A small inset picture at upper left shows threshing machines and 2,270 sacks of grain produced in 1901. This property and a parcel next to it, a total of 685 acres, were purchased by the Mohr family.

Mohr also had a strong interest in horses, being a breeder of Clydesdale stock and draft animals.

The Mohr house has been moved from its original location, and efforts are currently underway to find a way to restore it for use by the public. ALVHS Archives

Home Styles

Ann Doss, previous curator for the Amador-Livermore Valley Historical Society Museum, and Gary Drummond of the Livermore Heritage Guild, did work to identify the classic styles of homes in the valley.

One of the most common designs was the Queen Anne style. Here is a home built by Tom Knox in the 1890s on L Street in Livermore. It is said to be one of the finest homes of this type. Gary Drummond now resides there. ALVHS Archives

This is the side view of the Queen Anne, built in the 1880s on Sixth Street in Livermore. ALVHS Archives

This 1902 building was the Charles Graham residence in Pleasanton. Other examples of the Queen Anne style are at 4636 Second Street, 303 Neal Street, and 431 and 443 St. Mary Street. ALVHS Archives

This home in Livermore was built in 1898 and has been classified as Colonial Revival. ALVHS Archives

The Gothic Revival style is seen here in what is now the Pleasanton Century House Bicentennial Park on Santa Rita Road. It was dedicated in 1976, restored from a home built around 1878.

Other examples of Gothic Revival in Pleasanton are at 4466 and 4397 Second Street. The house at the latter address is similar to that of the Century House. ALVHS Archives

In Livermore at South Livermore Avenue and Fourth Street is the old Kennedy home (1878), an example of Gothic Revival. The two-story home visible at the rear and to the right is the Methodist Church parsonage. ALVHS Archives

Commercial Italianate or just Italianate can be seen in the Johnston Building, Kolln Hardware, and the new 450 Main restoration. Another example is the old Bank of Pleasanton/Gale Law Offices Building on Neal Street near the old Southern Pacific Depot.

An example in Livermore is the Charles Gardella home built in 1910. Here the family is posed in the yard. Business offices are now located in the building, moved from its original location to the present site. ALVHS Archives

The Bay Area Shingle Style was built from the 1880s through the 1920s. This house, located on L Street in Livermore, belonged to the Anspacher Brothers, who owned and operated warehouses and other businesses in the town. ALVHS Archives

Another of the large, mansion-like houses is the home of Elbert C. Apperson in Sunol. He and his wife Elizabeth purchased land there in 1873 and began building their home. It was finished in 1878 or 1879 according to descendent William W. Apperson who currently resides on St. Mary Street in Pleasanton with his wife Ann DeCastro Apperson.

Randolph W. Apperson, "Bill's" father, was born at Phoebe Apperson Hearst's Hacienda in 1897, now Castlewood Country Club. ALVHS Archives

Facing south and adjacent to Pleasanton Elementary School to the east on Minnie Street (once Pico and now Bernal) is the "old red house." From about 1900 to 1916 the Herman Koopmann family lived there and operated a dairy. Bertha Koopman, one of the women on the porch, kept house for her brother. Moller Family Photo

The Henry Moller home, built in 1916, is on Foothill Road north of Pleasanton near Dublin and the Stoneridge Shopping Center. It sat in an open field before construction of the slaughter-house, barns, and holding pens. The original meat business was across the road in the 1920s. It burned and the current site was completed in the 1940s. Moller Family Photo

During the wine boom of the 1880s it was fashionable for well-to-do San Franciscans to come to the valley, purchase land, build a large home, and farm or plant a vineyard. Many came by train for weekends and brought friends to entertain.

One such person was politician Christopher A. Buckley, who bought a hundred acres in 1885. Buckley called his country estate Ravenswood from a reminiscence of an experience on the East Coast. At his death in 1922, Ravenswood was taken over by the Redemptorist Fathers as a retreat and re-named Villa San Clemente.

The Livermore Area Recreation and Park District has now restored the building and the tankhouse. It hopes in the near future to complete a wine museum there. Currently the large building is used both for public and for private functions. Dopking Photo

Another view of Ravenswood shows some of the grounds around the large building, used mainly for entertaining when it was first built. ALVHS Archives

Not all homes built in the valley during the late 1800s and early 1900s were opulent showplaces. The smaller, average home was more the mode. Here is Hiram Bailey's house on L Street in Livermore. Janet Newton, author and artist, shows a watercolor done in the 1960s before the house was torn down. Bailey's wife was Robert Livermore's stepdaughter. LHG Photo

Built in 1860 near Livermore, the Galway home is an example of the typical farm residence and tankhouse. This picture of the property was taken about 1914. The property now belongs to the Moldt family. ALVHS Archives

The J. Schneider home, built on Main Street in Pleasanton, is an example of a modest home of 1893. The structure was located near what is now the Cheese Factory. The original picture is owned by his daughter and long-time local resident Lillie Fiorio. ALVHS Archives

Another turn of the century Pleasanton home on Main Street is that of Dr. William H. Cope. He is pictured on the porch with his wife Bertha. ALVHS Archives

As both Livermore and Pleasanton grew, large public or civic and commercial buildings began to appear. Built in 1905, the Sweeney Opera House was located at First and McLeod streets in Livermore. It burned in the mid 1940s but the front portion was saved. It was rebuilt and now is occupied by businesses. LHG Photo

The Masonic Building on First Street in Livermore (at the flagpole) was under construction around 1908. Sarboraria Photo

Shown here is the Masonic Building in the 1920s with businesses on both the first and second floors. The Schenone Building two doors away with the Bell Theatre is easily recognizable. A similar photo, taken from the other direction, appears in the business chapter. ALVHS Archives

Erected in 1880, this building was first the Livermore Bank, then briefly a hotel, and finally City Hall with the Fire Department alongside. Note the old bell and siren warning system on the roof tower. LHG Photo

In the 1930s, an attempt was made to enhance the looks of City Hall, and decorative stucco was added along with some interior renovation and a few new windows. LHG Photo

Livermore was the first town in California to establish a free public library, accomplished in 1874 entirely with citizen support. No tax money was used. Pictured here is the stately Carnegie Building, completed in 1911 to house the library.

It is now occupied by the Livermore Heritage Guild, Livermore Art Association, Livermore-Amador Genealogical Society, and the Livermore Woman's Club. Basement rooms are rented for meetings by the Livermore Recreation and Parks District. ALVHS Archives

The Bank of Italy (Bank of America) was located in this imposing cavernous structure on First Street in Livermore diagonally across from the flagpole. Built in 1920, it replaced the stately McLeod Building.

To the far right is one of the

N. D. Dutcher stores, and sandwiched in between is a building which contained in the 1920s according to local legend, a business which offered legally questionable services to its male clientele. Sarboraria Photo

In the 1930s, during the lean economic times, buildings like this one were erected by the WPA in communities everywhere. Here is the Veterans Memorial Building in Livermore. ALVHS Archives

In Pleasanton at the south end of Main Street is the Veterans Memorial Building, exhibiting the vast similarity in design for all such structures. Author Photo, 1988

The Pleasanton Women's Improvement Club sponsored and completed this building at the corner of Main and Division streets in 1914. It was also used as Town Hall (City Hall), Public Library, Police Department, and now the Amador-Livermore Valley Historical Society. ALVHS Archives

This old home, built in 1910 and located in the center of the Alameda County Fairgrounds, served as the fair administration building until 1971 when the Amador-Livermore Historical Society leased it to establish a museum. In 1984 the ALVHS leased the old Town Hall and spent a year and a half restoring it with much community help. The site opened in June of 1985. ALVHS Archives

Here is Pleasanton at the turn of the century with a graded gravel main street, dusty in the summer and muddy in the winter. It was not until about 1914 that paving was done, largely because Main Street had been designated as a county road. ALVHS Archives

Companies, Corporations and Other Large Endeavors

Phoebe Apperson Hearst had a grand manor on the ridge west of Pleasanton called the Hacienda del Pozo de Verona, remodeled from her late husband's hunting lodge and added to magnificently to a total of fifty rooms. An architect began work in 1891 to design the Spanish-Moorish Hacienda, and Phoebe moved to her completed home in 1899.

She entertained lavishly, having visitors come by Southern Pacific and Western Pacific from the Bay area through Niles Canyon to small stations she had built at the tracks in the valley below. She co-founded the PTA and also contributed to fifty or more schools and organizations. Her life came to an end in 1919 after a bout with influenza.

At this point the commercialization of the Hacienda began. In 1920, the first country club was formed, but the Great Depression of the 1930s put it under. John Marshall bought the property and opened what was to become the famous "dude ranch" in the 1930s and 1940s. The property was sold in the 1950s to a group that formed what is now Castlewood Country Club.

Phoebe A. Hearst is pictured here "prior to 1863." She was born in 1842 and married in 1862 to George Hearst, twenty-three years her senior. That would make her possibly twenty years old in this picture. ALVHS Archives

In later years at the Hacienda, this is Phoebe probably between 1900 and 1910. ALVHS Archives

This view of the front entrance of the Hacienda shows the circular fountain, shipped from Italy in 1902. Some sources date this picture at 1895, but Phoebe didn't move in until 1899, although she may have been residing on a partly completed portion of her new estate. The original photo belonged to William Apperson. Credit should also be given to John Edmands, an editor of the Pleasanton Times *now living in England. ALVHS Archives*

The rear of Hacienda del Pozo de Verona is pictured here in about 1899. ALVHS Archives

Pictured here is a closeup photo of the rear of the Hacienda in the 1920s. The first country club kept the planting in manicured condition. ALVHS Archives

*Casa Bonita, Phoebe's guest house, is shown in the late 1970s or early 1980s before it was torn down in 1982. ALVHS Archives—*Valley Times *Photo*

John A. Marshall II and his wife Edith are pictured seated in front of their sprawling home south of and above the main Hacienda. They were proprietors for "The West's Most Glamorous Dude Ranch" in the 1930s and 1940s which used the facilities of the Hearst Hacienda. This photo was taken in 1970 as Castlewood Country Club was being rebuilt following a disastrous fire the year before. The Marshalls had considerable input into the plans for new buildings. Bill Owens Photo

This scene is one looking down the entry road to the courtyard and from to the Hacienda, near the end of the dude ranch years in the 1940s. Dagmar Orloff Fulton Collection

The lush planting is shown near the courtyard entryway. Dagmar Orloff Fulton Collection

Pictured is an overview of Castlewood
Country Club in the 1950s on a warm
summer day with the pool crowded with
swimmers and sunbathers and the golf
course teeming with players. ALVHS
Archives

In a closer aerial view the club is seen in
winter with the pool partially drained.
This picture is from the late 1950s or
early 1960s. ALVHS Archives

In 1969 disaster struck Castlewood Country Club. A fire in the dead of night destroyed the main buildings of the historic Hacienda. Pictured is the morning aftermath, the smoking ruins. The Castlewood Board met almost immediately to rebuild the club in a more modern style than the original. It remains in operation today. ALVHS Archives

Early Industry and Mining

From 1862 through 1907 no fewer than nine coal mines were recorded in the Tesla area (Corral Hollow) east of Livermore. Historians refer to it as the boom of the 1870s, but according to some reports the coal was low grade lignite and veins were very thin. However, other reports said that at the 400-foot level the coal was of very good quality. The demise of the mines, then, was not due to poor quality but rather from the introduction of and use of oil where coal had been used previously. Of the large number of mines, none was successful and shortly after the turn of the century all had been closed. *ALVHS Archives*

These miners dug coal that was shipped to the San Francisco waterfront to fuel the steamships. Their jobs ended after 1900 when oil was introduced as an alternative energy source for the ships and industries. At the Tesla mine site there was a saloon, cottages, a hotel, a store, bunk houses, a library, a hospital, a barber, a tailor, a dairy, a cobbler, and a stable. *LHG Photo—Stockton Record*

110

About five miles back into Corral Hollow in Tesla the Carnegie Brick Company produced brick, fire brick, and vitreous china pieces for bathroom and kitchen, operating with coal from the nearby mines and using local clay. The brickworks operated during the same years as the mines. They were bought out in the 1890s by Treadwell Company, and finally closed about 1910. ALVHS Archives

Two other brickworks were in business at the turn of the century (still operating in 1911), the Remillard Brick Company about a half mile east of Pleasanton on the right side of what is now Stanley Boulevard and the Livermore Fire Brick Company on the west edge of Livermore across from what is now Valley Memorial Hospital. Neither exists today. Pictured here is the Livermore Fire Brickworks around 1900. ALVHS Archives

This picture of the Livermore Fire Brick Company is from the 1940s after it had been taken over by the Gladding-McBean Company. LHG Photo

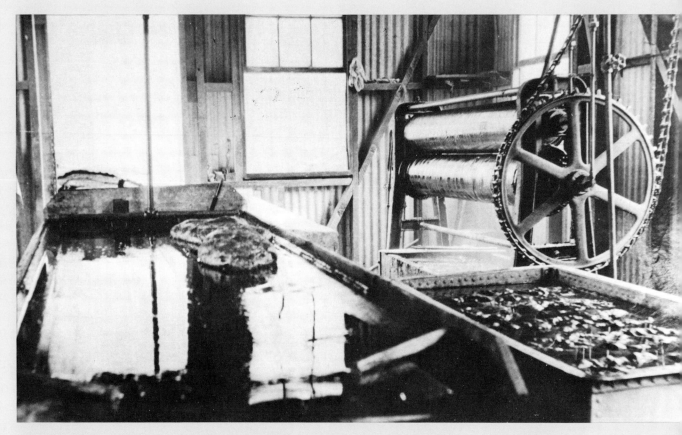

In 1913 the Coast Manufacturing Company began making explosives, fuses for military and industry uses, in the quiet, rural, safe Livermore community. Just east out First Street on the right is Trevarno Road, and a drive through that secluded street reveals today most of the residential buildings of seventy-five years ago.

Fuses were manufactured for both World War I and World War II, but in 1947 the company moved into the field of fiberglass. In 1954 Coast moved to Texas, and in the 1960s the "fuse works" became a branch of Hexcel Corp. LVHS Archives

In the late 1940s, Coast Manufacturing was using the machinery here to weave sheets of fiberglass onto large rolls for industrial uses. ALVHS Archives

This office of the many-faceted Hexcel Corporation is today located on Dublin Boulevard. Author Photo

Another major industry in the Dublin area is Foremost Research Center on Dublin Boulevard. This photo was taken in 1970. Among the work projects is extensive testing of new products with wide community involvement. DHPA Photo

the 1900s, George Jamieson had a al and wood business in Pleasanton nd organized what has become Rhodes nd Jamieson to supply gravel cement. he business then became a gravel eration. In 1923 Henry J. Kaiser founded Kaiser Sand and Gravel to pave the Pleasanton-Livermore Road (Stanley Boulevard). Since then Pacific Coast Aggregates opened (now Lone Star) along with several other smaller operations around Pleasanton. Pictured here is a 1955 aerial photo of a typical gravel excavation with digging, washing, separating, and loading machinery. Today gravel remains a thriving business. ALVHS Archives

In 1915, Henry Moller began a slaughter-house and meat packing business on Foothill Road northwest of Pleasanton (now near Stoneridge Mall). His three sons, Harold, Lloyd, and Roy, entered the business with their father when they graduated from high school in 1935, 1937, and 1940, respectively. Author Photo, 1988

The Moller brothers are seen in this 1960s picture preparing animal car-casses for shipment. The plant killed and prepared for market cattle, calves, swine, and sheep. Because of urban growth and problems with traffic and nearby neighbors, the movement of animals to the slaughterhouse for killing ceased in 1986. The business does, however, continue to do meat cutting and packing and distributes prepared meats from several sources. ALVHS Archives

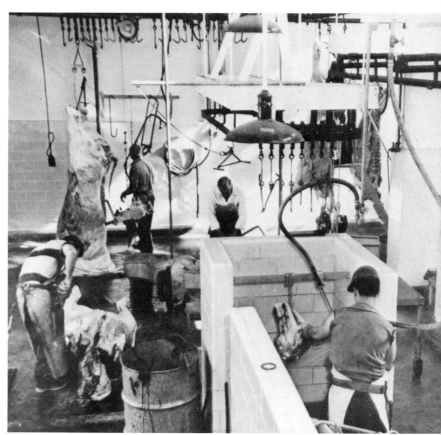

116

An annual event was the roundup in the Calaveras hills southeast of Pleasanton and east of Sunol. Leading the herd down the road are Janet Linfoot and Emmet Sulvian.

Resting the riders and the herd and holding the line is Alma Cronin Hall. This roundup was in the early 1950s. Moller Family Photos

A curious mixture of cattle, men on horseback, cars, and large trucks (Foothill Road west of Pleasanton) in the 1960s is a roundup scene that is gone forever. ALVHS Archives

The cooking crew gets lunch ready for the roundup riders. Left to right are Janet Linfoot, Alma Cronin Hall, Marie Cronin, Evelyn G. Moller, Edna Dobbel, Evelyn R. Moller, Margaret Mason, and Evelyn Hempe. Moller Family Photo

Working the meat plant in the late 1930s and 1940s is this staff: (left to right) Henry Moller (father), Harold Moller, Lloyd Moller, and Roy Moller (sons), California meat inspector Wilmot, Heine Koopmann, John Blasquez, and Al Martinez. Moller Family Photo

118

*During World War II a naval air train-
ing station operated east of Livermore.
These buildings later became the first
facilities for the new Lawrence Livermore Laboratory. ALVHS Archives*

North of Pleasanton across what was then Highway 50 (now Interstate 580) Camp Parks (Shoemaker) was commissioned in 1943 and closed in 1946. The thousand bed naval hospital there served during World War II. Camp Parks was reactivated in the early 1950s for the Korean conflict.

The base was a Construction Battalion Replacement Depot, a part of Shoemaker Naval Training and Distribution Center, the largest station for Seabee personnel. In 1959 it was transferred to the U. S. Army. In modern times it will be the base for a new training center for a medical unit, similar to the well-known MASH contingents.
Herald *Photo*

Camp Shoemaker (Parks) during World War II had many functions, one of which was for WAVES (Women Appointed for Voluntary Emergency Service), also known as the Women's Reserve of the United States Naval Reserve. Pictured here in 1943 are bus loads of WAVES leaving Shoemaker for duty overseas, transportation provided by the Twelfth Naval District Transportation Pool, Treasure Island, San Francisco. Local resident Frieda Steffenauer supervised over four hundred drivers who bused thousands of military personnel for shipment overseas during wartime. Frieda Helgesen Steffenauer *Photo*

he arrival of two "atomic energy" boratories on the east edge of Livermore in the 1950s brought more population and economic changes than any ther influence in this century. Lawnce Livermore (National) Laboratory, tablished in 1952, is a research and evelopment facility whose primary ork is the design of nuclear weapons.

It has also maintained programs in peaceful technology. Today about eighty-five hundred are employed there.

Sandia National Labs, across the street on East Avenue, began in 1956 as an engineering support group for L.L.N.L. weapons work. Its main mission is research and development on the non-nuclear parts of weapons. A per-

centage of its programs are combustion energy research. Sandia employs about eleven hundred.

L.L.N.L. is operated today by the University of California for the United States Department of Energy. Sandia is owned by A.T. & T. but also is funded by the D.O.E. Courtesy of Barry Schrader

This is one of the earliest aerial photos of the quickly developing facilities at Lawrence Livermore (National) Laboratory. The old naval air station barracks and other buildings of the base are readily discernible. ALVHS Archives

This aerial view of the "Lab" was taken in 1969, indicating considerable growth and construction of new buildings. ALVHS Archives

Pictured here is the main Sandia building in 1959, used for administration and personnel. Courtesy of Sandia Public Information

General Electric Company purchased a site in 1956 south and east of Livermore/Pleasanton but nearer to Sunol for its Vallecitos Nuclear Center (V.N.C.). Three years later reactor test programs were completed for the world's largest privately financed nuclear research facility. Sarboraria Photo

From 1958 through 1964 prototype nuclear reactor testing brought about the first licensed commercial reactor to make electricity. The reactor produced five megawatts of power for Pacific Gas and Electric Company from 1959 through 1963. A second area of work was materials testing which was done in a reactor from 1958 through 1978. The reactor was closed down but testing continues today. A third area of work was the production of medical products which started in 1964 and ended in 1978. ALVHS Archives and Robert Butler

In Livermore, around 1914, drainage and sewer lines were being completed to prepare for the paving that was to come. Here shown is First Street which also had been designated as a state highway. LHG Archives

Typical on rural roads and state high-ways is this bridge which made one of the several crossings of the Arroyo del Valle between Pleasanton and Sunol. This photo was taken probably in the 1940s. Photo Courtesy of Dagmar Fulton

Here in 1988 is an east-facing view of a bridge crossing the Arroyo del Valle between Pleasanton and Sunol. The crossover road from Foothill Road to Pleasanton-Sunol Road has been closed to vehicles and the floor of the bridge finished as a pedestrian and cycle way. The rustic quality of the rural scene remains. Author Photo

This aerial view of the Amador-Livermore Valley in 1955 shows Livermore in the foreground beginning to grow, Pleasanton at upper left, and Dublin at upper right. The old highway 50 (Stockton Road of Lincoln Highway) can be seen cutting diagonally from upper center to the right side of the picture. That highway was soon to become Freeway 580. ALVHS Archives

The Pleasanton area in 1967-1968 was experiencing rapid expansion in home building to the north and west and to the south and east. The new Freeway 680 can be seen cutting across the top of the picture from left to right. ALVHS Archives

A sign of the times in 1965 is a section of 580 Freeway being completed. This view is looking west as the road rises on old highway 50 up the Dublin Grade. With two major freeways completed, north and south and east and west, crossing each other at Dublin, the time was right for major commercial and residential development in the valley. ALVHS Archives

The Amador-Livermore Valley abounds in "clean" industry. Operating in 1970 was Kaiser Center for Technology. It remains a viable part of the community south of Pleasanton. Author Photo

This is the driveway through landscaped grounds to Kaiser.

What was once the West Coast distribution center for Scholastic Books is now the regional offices for Denny's and Proficient Food Company.

Harper and Row Publishers was housed here in the 1970s. Today it is occupied by Nu Dex and Scientific Services.
Author Photos

The 1980s have brought the greatest
expansion for hotels, office space,
residential development, and retail
businesses in the history of the valley. A
hundred years ago this area was a
willow swamp, drained partly in the
summer and planted in hops. Today it is
Hacienda Business Park. Author Photo.

To the west of all the new business park
development across Freeway 680 and at
the foot of the Pleasanton Ridge foothills
is Stoneridge Mall. At the present time, it
boasts anchor store names of Penney's,
Emporium Capwell, and Macy's, as well
as two interior levels of retail shops.
Author Photo

Two other developing business parks are Koll Center, southwest of Pleasanton, and Meyer, directly west of Hacienda. Author Photos

Winter rains drained from hills to the east of Pleasanton down into the valley and ended in a large swampy area which stretched from the town all the way west and north almost to Dublin. This photo was taken in 1955 on the right side of Hopyard Road where the sports park is now located.

From the center and off to the right all the way to Freeways 580 and 680 the area was covered with water. Hacienda Business Park now occupies the land. Large drains have been dug and water moves south along the Arroyo to Sunol and through Niles Canyon to the Bay. ALVHS Archives

On the other side of town out Santa Rita Road the 1955 flood was also evident. Here water covers the farm land in the vicinity of Mohr Avenue. ALVHS Archives

Popularity of the July 4 Parade down Main Street in Pleasanton at the turn of the century is evident in this much-published picture. The crowd surges out into the street to greet this popular float passing by. Dust is rising in the distance from the unpaved street as the horses and various forms of wagons and buggies move along the street. ALVHS Archives

Parades, Fairs, Rodeos, and Festivals

Independence Day has always been the time for community celebrations, as has been fall harvest time, the county fair, heritage observances, or any reason at all (Good Times Roll Parades), and let's not forget the valley-wide wine tastings.

Pictures in the following series illustrate in some measure part of those summer observances which centered on and around the Fourth of July with fairs, rodeos, and patriotic parades.

PLEASANTON RACE TRACK.

Agostin Bernal built a track as early as 1850, and by 1885 the track and the horses it trained were known nationwide. Over the years, the facility was owned by several interests. Here from an early drawing is the raceway and residence of Joseph F. Nevis, who took over operation of the track in 1878. ALVHS Archives, Thompson and West Historical Atlas

This view of the Alameda County Fairgrounds in the 1950s or before shows the trotting track inside the full racetrack, the antiquated circular exhibit buildings near the entrance, the old lineup of horse barns (upper center), the Court of the Four Seasons, but none of the new additions which make up the grounds today. ALVHS Archives

Over the years the race track grand-stand was improved and made larger several times. Here it is pictured in the 1920 viewed looking west toward the barns situated to the rear and to the left. ALVHS Archives

To some, the Alameda County Fair-grounds was only the race track. However, technically it has always been an agricultural fair with exhibits of all kinds of crops, machinery, preserved foods, millinery, hobbies, and crafts. This photo shows the rather primitive exhibit buildings built in 1912 by the original Fair Commission, founders of the Alameda County Fair.

Today the fair Administration Building on Pleasanton Avenue stands where this structure was. The original building served in its final years as the 4-H Building and also housed a model railroad club. ALVHS Archives

It's advertising for the July 4 Parade and the usual young folks (pretty girls) are out creating some noise to draw attention to the fair, the annual parade, or possibly a barbeque or a dance. The A. B. Casterson family makes up most of the group here in around 1900, probably at the corner of Main Street and Angela Avenue in front of Charlie Schween's house. ALVHS Archives

The Alameda County Fair opened in 1912 for a run of October 23-27. A seventy-five-year celebration was held in 1987. This 1939 photo shows that the old exhibit buildings were still standing, but the growth of commercialism is evident with stall booths selling food, refreshments, souvenirs, and entertainment. ALVHS Archives

Typical of the annual Alameda County Fair floats is this one which appeared in the late 1940s in a Livermore Rodeo Parade. Dopking Photo

Most communities in Alameda County have a "Day at the Races." Here in the early 1960s are Dublin Day representatives in the winner's circle in front of the grandstand at the Alameda County Fair in Pleasanton. Moller Family Photo

In the early 1950s, the Volunteer Fire Department jeep is pulling a bevy of beauties on the Pleasanton Lions Club float down Main Street in the annual

"Parade Capital's" extravaganza prior to the Alameda County Fair. ALVHS Archives

One of the many youth floats in an annual Alameda County Fair Parade of the 1960s is this Camp Fire Girls, District II, group. For those who have been around for a few years, remember May's Dress Shop (Millinery) and P and X Market (also Hagstrom's and County Fair)? Author Photo

In a salute to Pleasanton senior citizens, Joe Antonini drives Al Casterson and Norma Kolln in his antique car in an Alameda County Fair Parade. Author Photo

Getting ready for Pleasanton's seventy-fifth birthday (1894-1969) are (left to right) Rose Bernard, Julie Dunham, Ruth Thomas, Peggy Plato, and Gerry Nerton of the Business and Professional Women's Club. They are shown with vehicles of Howard Hansen's antique car collection. The celebration lasted for two weeks and included a ball, a maid contest, fashion show, mural unveiling, fire apparatus parade and water competition, square dance, winetasting, bike races, Little League playoffs, flea market, pancake breakfast, and the Fair Parade. Author Photo

The "Good Times Roll Parade" came to Pleasanton in 1974 as further testimony and evidence to the claim of the "Parade Capital" title. Exemplifying the relaxed humor of the event is the Balloon Platoon, formed for the parade and riding in a Viking ship (Ship Clyde) being towed down Main Street. That wouldn't do, so in 1975 the group began to march and do comedy routines on the street. Here in 1987 is the group at "shoulder arms—mops" finishing its show in front of the reviewing stand in the Alameda County Fair Parade. Author Photo

Stepping up to the competition line is the Dublin High School Marching Band. This photo was taken at a Dublin Festival Parade of the late 1960s.

Bands in the valley have played a major role in annual modern times parades and celebrations, including the Foothill Band Review in Pleasanton, Heritage Days Parade in Pleasanton, Rodeo Parade in Livermore, Alameda County Fair Parade in Pleasanton, Good Times Roll Parade, the Holy Ghost Parade, as well as the Dublin Festival.

Competing for honors have been Livermore High School, Granada High School, Amador Valley High School, Foothill High School, and Dublin High School. The modern expansion began in the 1960s with Chan Henderson's Pleasanton Elementary School Tartan Band and his "little army." Of course, both Livermore and Pleasanton had marching bands as early as the late 1800s. A modern counterpart of the Henderson bands today is the group from Wells Intermediate, an annual award winner. Author Photo

The Pioneer Folk Festival of 1985 is celebrated in Sunol Regional Park. The semi-annual event features a pie baking contest. Sunolian Photo

Volunteers Sue Plotkin, Harvey Wells, Susan Bledsoe, and naturalist Paul Ferreira work at the Pioneer Folk Festival. Sunolian Photo

The annual bed race is a main competition in Sunol. Here Addie's Town House entry has suffered a collapsed wheel. Sunolian Photo

Looking on is the Mayor of Sunol, Bosco "Boss" Ramos. The local newspaper, the Sunolian, *ran an election in August of 1981 and Bosco was the winner. Sunolian Photo*

Meanwhile, back in Livermore, the 1905 dedication of the new flagpole was a big downtown event. In this photo, ceremonies are taking place in the area between the flagpole and the old Livermore Hotel. LHG Phohto

Posed in grand style in front of the Sweeney Opera House in Livermore are the horse show directors around 1906. Sarboraria Photo

It's the Independence Day Parade along First Street in Livermore. This photo shows the Goddess of Liberty float in 1913 or before. ALVHS Archives

In 1914 the Druids had a convention in Livermore. Druids of the time were men, although the group did have a Women's Auxiliary. The ceremony here is in front of the flagpole with the McLeod Building behind. ALVHS Archives

About 1910 in the annual July 4 Parade in Livermore, the Ark Club, a group of local businessmen, entered this float. The story goes that the Ark (Sprig) was a boathouse on the San Joaquin River that sank every year with the winter high water. Men of the hunting club grew tired of re-floating it every year so they bought a small island in the river, and moved it to high ground. The Livermore Yacht Club is located in the same area. Sarboraria Photo

The Livermore Rodeo Parade began in 1919 as a Red Cross benefit and became an annual event. In this photo, the parade heads down First Street toward the flag pole and Mill Square. Dopking Photo.

VERMORE RODEO -:-

24 Spectacular EVENTS 24

onc Riding : : Brahma Steer Riding : : Calf
ping : : Single Roping : : Double Roping
eer Decorating : : Stockhorse Contests
ackamore Class : : Trick Riding : : Trick
ping : : Relay Races : : Free-For-All Races
ny Express Races : : Roman Races
ockhorse Races : : Wild Horse Races
And Many Other Special Events

◆

TICKET INFORMATION

served Seats	$1.50, $1.75, $2.25
neral Admission	85c
aildren, in General Admission, Sunday only	40c

CHILDREN FREE JUNE 8
If Accompanied by Adult
All seats in covered grandstand.
All prices include tax.

◆

For reservations or other information,
Write, Wire or Phone

LIVERMORE RODEO ASSN.
Phone Livermore 303
Livermore, California

HONORARY PRESIDENTS
John McGlinchey   Thos. W. Norris

DIRECTORS

R. P. Bernhardt, President	Al Bonne
	J. S. Concannon
	F. P. Cardosa
R. E. Merritt, Vice-President	R. A. Hansen
	M. R. Henry
	E. E. Johnson
M. G. Callaghan, Secretary	A. F. Kirschner
	C. G. Owens
	L. E. Van Patten
M. J. Clark, Treasurer	H. L. Wente
	H. S. Walker

This program for the 1835-1935 Centennial Livermore Rodeo celebration reveals what family entertainment was like a little over fifty years ago. The two-day festivities were a parade on Saturday, June 8, and the rodeo the next day. ALVHS Archives

The annual Livermore Rodeo and July 4 Parade was found to be too hot for competition and marching. So the date was moved to a bit cooler time in June. Here is the grand entry into the rodeo grounds in the 1930s. ALVHS Archives

At the rodeo grounds in 1919, the horse entries have formed a circle in the center of the field for a panoramic photo. The photo identifies the event as the "annual rodeo" on July 4. ALVHS Archives

In the 1930s, the Livermore Rodeo queen steps from her stagecoach. It is all part of the advertising to create public interest in the annual celebration. Sarboraria Photo

Here are local cowgirls advertising the annual Livermore Rodeo in 1949. The gimmick for that year was a centennial observance of the Gold Rush to California. Dopking Photo

In 1969, another rodeo centennial was celebrated. Vintage rail cars and stages were brought in, and people were encouraged to dress in the costume of the time. The city began in 1869 with the railroad and the laying out of the first portion of town along First Street. There was also a train trip in vintage cars. *Dopking Photo*

In the 1950s, this comic entry appeared in the annual parade in Livermore. R. A. Hansen had a car collection and for years appeared in the parade. *Dopking Photo*

Also in the 1950s, near First and J streets in Livermore, it seems as if dad is having some difficulty keeping the ponies and his two sons straight on the parade route. Dopking Photo

This timeless photo at the Livermore Rodeo could have been taken any year over the last seventy or so. Riding the bucking bronco has always attracted keen competition. Dopking Photo

Women's suffrage was an issue from the mid 1800s until 1920 when the Nineteenth Amendment to the Constitution was ratified. Here, probably in about 1918, a group of local women demonstrate their feelings about that issue or possibly some other one. Photo courtesy of Dagmar Orloff Fulton

At the opposite end of the historical spectrum is this photo of a mini parade in the 1960s celebrating the selection of Pleasanton as the site for the next California State College. The way it turned out, Hayward improved its financial share offering and Governor Edmond Brown yielded, thus changing the selection committee recommendation to Hayward. There are still people in the valley upset about it. Dopking Photo

Parades come in all forms and sizes. Here in about 1915 is Company I, California National Guard, the proud unit of the Amador-Livermore Valley, marching in Livermore down First Street. The unit existed for seventeen years with five hundred men from Livermore and Pleasanton serving. The Sweeney Opera House was used as an armory for Company I. It also served as a town meeting place for dances, basketball games, and even skating. Fire destroyed the building in the 1940s. ALVHS Archives

This formal picture shows part of the Company I contingent. The company was called to active duty four times: for the 1906 San Francisco earthquake and fire; the 1912 fire on Mt. Tamalpais in Marin County; in 1916 on the Mexican border in Arizona against Pancho Villa; and in France in World War I. Sarboraria Photo

Bands and music have always been important. But music for the schools received its biggest boost in the Pleasanton area when J. Chandler Henderson formed his Tartan Band in the 1960s made up of seventh and eighth graders (even a few grades five and six) at Pleasanton Elementary School.

His bands over the years performed in parades and at events around the Bay Area and, more importantly, fed young musicians into the high school. There developed through teaching in the high school and experience brought from the elementary a period of performing band excellence in the 1970s at Amador High School.

From those years there came fine bands from Livermore and Granada High Schools, Dublin High School, and the new Foothill High School. The annual Foothill Band Review steps off each fall down Main Street in Pleasanton with representative schools from Northern California and even a few from Southern California.

The Chan Henderson Bandstand is testimony to the band music in the valley. It is in the park at First and Neal streets, location of Friday Concerts in the Park which are performed annually all summer. Author Collection

Chapter 7

Churches, Schools, Hospitals and Fire Departments

The intent of this section on churches is to show the beginnings of the congregations in the valley from 1860 through the turn of the century. Space does not permit a catalog of the many denominations formed in the last sixty years or so.

Early churches of the valley include St. Raymond's Catholic Church of Dublin, St. Michael's Catholic Church of Livermore, St. Augustine's Catholic Church of Pleasanton, First Presbyterian Church of Livermore, Presbyterian Community Church of Pleasanton, Methodist Church of Livermore, and Congregational Church of Sunol Glen.

St. Raymond's Catholic Church parish was formed in 1860, and existed for years with a pastor who came from the Hayward area to observe masses. This is the church building in the late 1960s after it had been restored by the Amador-Livermore Historical Society. It sits alongside a restored version of Murray School, now the museum for the Dublin Historical Preservation Association. ALVHS Archives

First Presbyterian Church of Livermore had services as early as 1866 in the Laddsville school. The congregation was officially organized in 1871, the church building was dedicated in 1874, and an annex was added in 1890, which increased the capacity to five hundred. Dopking Photo

154

First Presbyterian Church is seen here at a later time. LHG Photo

First Presbyterian Church had improvements in the 1930s. LHG Photo

St. Michael's Catholic Church parish was formed in 1878 after ceasing to be dependent upon Mission San Jose, the chapel having been built in 1875 as a mission. Pictured is the original church at the turn of the century, located on First Street north of Mill Square (flagpole). LHG Photo

A fire destroyed St. Michael's Catholic Church on August 4, 1916. Today a Kinney Shoe Store is located on the site. ALVHS Archives

Construction of a new St. Michael's Catholic Church was underway in 1916-18 at the new location of Fourth and Maple streets next to the new parish school. Dopking Photo

The new mission style church was completed in 1918 and remains in use today. ALVHS Archives

This very early photo of St. Augustine's Catholic Church on Rose Avenue in Pleasanton was probably taken in the 1890s. The structure was demolished in the late 1960s and a new, modern structure erected on East Angela Street by 1969. St. Augustine's was a mission parish in 1882 with the original church built in that year. The first permanent pastor was assigned in 1901. ALVHS Archives

This late 1890s photo of St. Augustine's Catholic Church was taken looking east down Rose Avenue toward the center of town and Main Street. DHPA Photo

Construction of the United Presbyterian Community Church on Neal Street in Pleasanton was underway in 1876. This old photo is thought to have been taken about 1900. ALVHS Archives

This photo of United Presbyterian Community Church was taken between 1920 and 1930. The quality of this picture is better, but the structure has changed little except for paint and improved grounds. A new church and a Christian Education building were constructed on Mirador Drive. The Neal Street site is now occupied by Amador Valley Baptist Church. ALVHS Archives

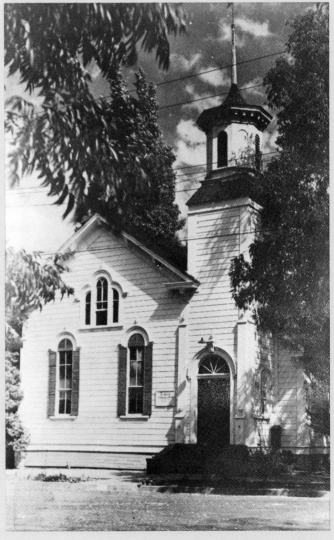

What was to become Asbury Methodist Episcopal Church in Livermore began as early as 1867 with a small group gathering at a home for worship. In 1868 meetings were held in a large hall along with the Presbyterians. In 1870 William Mendenhall donated a lot for a church building and parsonage. The church officially adopted its name in 1883 and construction of the building was completed the next year. In 1956 the congregation voted for the current site on East Avenue. ALVHS Archives

The M. E. (Methodist Episcopal) Church of Pleasanton was dedicated in 1888. The drawing shows a four-room parsonage and the sanctuary located on St. Mary Street. First services had begun ten years earlier with meetings in a home. ALVHS Archives

Something must have happened to the original church site because I.O.O.F. (Odd Fellows) Hall is also known to have been the meeting place for the Methodist Episcopal Church of Pleasanton. Location of the "club building" is on St. Mary Street, south side, no more than a hundred feet from Main Street. It continues in use today as the Church of Divine Man. The new Episcopal Church is now located on Hopyard Road. On the ground floor of the club building over the years were Joe's Grocery, Express Liquors, and a delicatessen and pizza take-out. ALVHS Archives

The Congregational Church of Sunol Glen, built in 1885, was originally white. Pictured here is the church in the late 1800s. ALVHS Archives

Today it is The Little Brown Church of Sunol. This photo was taken in 1974 and shows great care and upkeep for the structure. ALVHS Archives

The first school in the Amador-Livermore Valley was Murray School in Dublin in 1856. Shown here is most of a photo taken about 1890. The next schools established here were in Pleasanton in 1864, Sunol in 1865, and Laddsville (forerunner to Livermore) in 1866. Murray, like most of the first schools, was a one-room building. It had thirteen pupils. Dopking Photo

Coming down the steps at Murray School in 1949 are (left to right) Lynn Moller, John Banke, and Carolyn Wing. The school was located on old Dublin Road northwest of town. Moller Family Photo

Murray School was relocated next to Old St. Raymond's Catholic Church on Donlon Way. It was used on its original site by the Primitive Baptist Church, who added the room seen at the right in this photo. The building today houses the Dublin Historical Preservation Association. Author Photo

Pleasanton (Grammar) School was built in the 1860s and the second story rented to the Masons, Pleasanton Lodge 219, in 1871 because the space was not needed by the school at that time. A fire destroyed the building in 1910 and a new school was rebuilt on the same site. John Kottinger was the first president of the school board. This side view shows the student body in 1908. ALVHS Archives

This view of Pleasanton Grammar School is from the other side of the building about 1900. ALVHS Archives

After the 1910 fire a new school was built as seen in this early 1950s photo. It was torn down shortly after to make room for larger and more modern structures. Author Collection

The graduation class of Pleasanton Grammar School in 1906. The young man second from the right is holding the rolled diploma, a picture of which is seen below. Courtesy of Betty Winn Kozlowski

This watermarked diploma measuring a large twelve by eighteen inches was earned by Hiram Winn at Pleasanton School in 1906. It was awarded by the Alameda County Board of Education, C. L. Biedenbach, President. The principal at the time was Arthur E. Weed. Courtesy of Betty Winn Kozlowski

A new grammar school was completed on Fifth Street in Livermore in 1877. This is the new building ready to be occupied. ALVHS Archives

The public school on Fifth Street had to have an addition to make room for the influx of students from a growing Livermore in the 1890s. In 1896 the school had an enrollment of over five hundred and thirteen teachers. The present school was built in 1922. Sarboraria Photo

St. Michael's Catholic Church Convent and School was dedicated in September 1913. The school, located at Fourth and Maple streets, was spared by the fire that destroyed the original church in 1916. The school continues to operate today. ALVHS Archives

When the first Union High School in California opened in Livermore in 1891, it spelled the demise of Livermore College, founded in 1870 and serving about fifty students. It closed in 1893 because with the opening of the new high school there was no need for a private school. A fire in 1930 severely damaged the building, and it was torn down.

One-fifth of the enrollment in the public school consisted of students from Pleasanton. They commuted to school on horseback, by buggy, and even by train.

This historic first public high school was on Seventh Street but was torn down in 1930 because a new, larger one was to open. Sarboraria Photo

The new Livermore Union High School (home of the Cowboys) opened in 1930. In 1938 the handsome brick structure was made earthquake proof by the W.P.A. (Works Progress Administration) with federal funds. A second campus, Granada High School, has since opened. *Sarboraria Photo*

Some high school classes were taught in Pleasanton prior to the opening of Amador Valley Joint Union High School on Santa Rita Road in 1924. This building has since been razed and new facilities constructed. A remodeled auditorium remains. A second campus, Foothill High School, is also open for Pleasanton students. A third high school in Dublin is now part of a new district. *ALVHS Archives*

During the summer of 1968, demolition of the old Amador High School main building was started and completed. Author Photos

*George "Pat" Patterson shows off his
1932 Amador Valley Joint Union High
School of Pleasanton basketball team.
Pat was an institution at Amador,
coaching several sports over the years, as
well as teaching mathematics and
mechanical drawing. The football field
is named in his honor. Moller Family
Photo*

As the farm population of the Amador-Livermore Valley grew from the 1860s and into the 1900s, small, one or two-room rural schools were built to serve the outlying children. As the valley continued to change, these schools were abandoned and left to the elements.

Pictured here is Sunol Grammar School about 1911. ALVHS Archives

May School, located on Dagnino Road near Livermore, opened in the 1870s with one or two teachers and served children from outlying farms. It is typical of abandoned rural schools. Dopking Photo

*Another abandoned rural school of the
past is located in the countryside near
Altamont. This photo was taken in 1973.
Dopking Photo*

Typical of the revered school teachers of the late 1800s and early 1900s is Elisabeth Flanagan Nevin (1883-1958) of Dublin. She was a Murray School teacher in 1901 and later. ALVHS Archives

May Nissen taught English and Latin at Livermore High School from 1910 through 1948. Pictured here in the 1960s, she is being honored at First Presbyterian Church as a speaker about the importance of her family. Left to right are Herbert Hagemann, Roger Brown, May Nissen (seated left), Janet Newton (pouring), and Jim Nissen. LHG Photo

ven after the turn of the century, ealth care in the valley was provided in amily homes or a doctor's office. In ivermore, Mamie Aylward, a nurse, ared for the sick and injured at a ouse rented from Susie Kelly on Street in 1910. Tonsils were even emoved there, but those with serious nesses or needing other care had to go Alameda, Oakland, or San Francisco.

A room at City Hall was reserved for ersons with communicable diseases he old concept of "pest house") or for stranger who might have an accident town. A Dr. Cutler in the 1870s had e first drug store on First Street near ill Square.

Several small hospitals opened: 1918-925 on Second Street, another on the orner of Fifth and L streets in 1926, nd still another in 1927 to care for etch-Hetchy workers who were injured orking on the water project.

Dr. Paul Dolan and a nurse, Miss lbertson, began care of the ill and jured in 1925 and opened St. Paul's

Hospital as a private facility with 23 beds in 1927. Today it is a nursing home.

In 1958 fundraising began in the valley for a new hospital and in 1961 Valley Memorial Hospital opened with

46 beds. In 1969 a third floor was added, increasing the capacity to 110 beds. Other improvements have been completed, and plans are now under-way for a second facility in north Pleasanton. ALVHS Archives.

In 1895, Dr. John W. Robertson chose Livermore as the site for a sanitarium for the treatment of "nervous dyspeptics, neurasthenics, and general disease" away from the home setting. Patients resided at the sanitarium for a therapy of diet, exercise, water and other mas-sage, and quiet sunny surroundings.

Four cottages were also provided for patients with "mental diseases."

Shown in this overview is the Liver-more Sanitarium grounds on College Avenue. The photo is of poor quality but does show some of the buildings before 1920. ALVHS Archives

175

The home of Dr. Robertson was at College and L streets and part of the sanitarium. Sarboraria Photo

This imposing structure was referred to as the "hydro," housing facilities for water massage and treatment in several forms. A gymnasium was also a part of the building in the Livermore Sanitarium complex. Dopking Photo

An earlier view of the hydro is shown here. The sanitarium is said to have had accommodations for eighty-five patients. ALVHS Archives

Photo Courtesy of Valley Memorial Hospital

177

In 1918, a site was chosen in the dry climate of the valley near Livermore for the Arroyo Del Valle Sanitorium, a hospital to treat tuberculous patients. It had accommodations for about two hundred adults and children. The facility ceased to operate after a better cure for tuberculosis was found.

Here is another view of the sanitorium, called in this photo "Del Valle Ranch." ALVHS Archives

As part of the Del Valle Sanitorium, the Alameda County Tuberculosis Association established this Del Valle Farm for Children on five acres of land in 1921 and by 1922 the first building had been erected. The farm was financed through the sale of Christmas Seals. Courtesy of Sally Bystroff

About ten miles southeast of Livermore at the 1,750 foot elevation on Cedar Mountain is Mendenhall Springs. According to the advertising of the times it was a place to go to rest and drink water which was a lightly carbonated tonic, antacid, diuretic, and laxative. Of course, in the 1890s many types of medication were claimed as cure-alls.

Pictured is the bus to Mendenhall Springs. It would pick up passengers in several parts of town and transport them to the springs for the day or for an overnight stay at several cabins which could be rented. *LHG Photo*

High in the hills at Mendenhall Springs was this "cottage," one of several to rent for overnight stays to be near the "healthful" water. *Sarboraria Photo*

In 1924, the federal government chose a site near Livermore for a hospital to treat tuberculosis and other medical cases. It is the United States Veterans' Bureau Hospital, No. 102, often referred to as the Veterans Administration Hospital. Located five miles south of town, it continues to operate today. This first photo is from 1925, showing the main building nearing completion. Dopking Photo

In this aerial view from 1930 or later of the Veterans Hospital, it seems as if the vineyards in the foreground of the older picture have been allowed to disappear. ALVHS Archives

Hose Carts, Volunteers, Engines, and Stations

In 1874 the first fire fighting unit was formed in the valley, Hook and Ladder Company No. 1 in Livermore. The city incorporated in 1876 with Fire Company No. 1 forming. A fire station was built at Second and L streets. In 1888 a thousand pound bell was added and used to summon volunteers. The first gasoline powered vehicle was purchased in 1916—a Model T Ford truck.

In 1888 the Pleasanton Fire Department was organized as a volunteer unit with three companies and twenty men. The first firehouse was built in the early 1900s as a tower with a twenty-seven hundred pound bell and small shed for equipment. The Fire Department was officially established in 1901. In 1928, a brick firehouse was built on the old station site.

This picture of the Pleasanton Fire Department volunteers with their hose cart was taken in Livermore in 1901 after a July 4 parade and race competition. Pleasanton won. The firemen are identified as George Jamison, George W. Nelson, Dan Madsen, Charles S. Graham, Lee Wells, Will Ludwig, Will Graham, Bert Frost, Arthur Ralph, W. P. Martin, Charles Pingre, and A. B. Pickard (spelling not guaranteed). ALVHS Archives

At about the same time the Pleasanton Volunteers placed their cart on a horse-drawn wagon for another parade, probably again in Livermore. ALVHS Archives

In this slightly out-of-focus picture from a Main Street Parade in Pleasanton in the early 1900s the Volunteer Fire Department comes down the street with its hose cart. ALVHS Archives

Pictured here in 1974 is a group of paid and volunteer firemen pulling ancient equipment in a Pleasanton parade which had Fire Muster competition that day. For years a street was closed off (Main or Neal) and teams from departments from cities in Northern California would compete in pumping contests and races using vintage apparatuses. ALVHS Archives

The Pleasanton station burned in 1927, bringing about construction of a new one on the same site on Railroad Avenue. ALVHS Archives

By 1929, this new building was complete. Bricks were used from the Remillard Brick Company, located at the time just northeast of town on what is now Stanley Boulevard. At that time it was referred to as Pleasanton-Livermore Road. ALVHS Archives

Shown here is Livermore City Hall after it had been remodeled with a new coat of stucco. The fire department is alongside. In 1920 a pumper was purchased which served for forty years before it was taken out of service. Dopking Photo

In 1916, the Livermore Fire Department purchased a Model T Ford truck/engine, the first motorized vehicle for the department. Here it is parked by Beck's Drug Store on K Street. Sarboraria Photo

In the 1920s the Pleasanton Fire Department purchased several vehicles, a mixture of America La France, Cadillac, Mason Road King, and Star-Durant. Pictured here is one of those. The building behind was not identified. ALVHS Archives

In 1945, the Pleasanton Fire Department was still a volunteer group. Standing center is John J. Amaral, the last volunteer fire chief, along with some of his firemen. The engine at the left has long since been retired and is now a Pleasanton Jaycees vehicle used for parades and other events. From 1963 to 1965 the department changed with a fulltime chief and hired firemen. The volunteers continue to be active today. *ALVHS Archives*

Standing jauntily in front of the Ratti French and Italian Restaurant on Main Street in Pleasanton is John J. Amaral as a young man. He was employed at the time as a waiter or bartender (a difficult job since it was probably during Prohibition). The interesting part of all this is that Mr. and Mrs. Ratti had four eligible daughters, and Johnny married one, Ruth, in 1927. Both, now deceased, were community leaders for over fifty years. Photo courtesy of Geraldine Ratti "Chidge" Nerton

In the 1890s the Bohemian Club, a group
of local Livermore area businessmen,
used this isolated spot on Brushy Peak as
a party place. Along with the many stories

of bandits in the valley, Joaquin Murieta
was supposed to have used the place as
one of his hideouts. Dopking Photo

Chapter 8

A Potpourri of People and Places

In a valley-wide sampling of history through pictures, some type of organization must be assumed, as in this manuscript of pictures and illustrations.

However, many good photos did not find their rightful places in the preceding pages of settlers, farming, business, homes, industry, celebrations, churches, fire departments, hospitals, and schools.

In the section that follows, there are groups, some family photos, a movie star, a famous writer, dedications, parties, and just people.

One source said 1913, another 1915-16, for the filming of the movie Rebecca of Sunnybrook Farm *in Pleasanton. This photo is a copy of one autographed by Mary Pickford. Dopking Photo*

Mary Pickford is shown here as a scene is filmed with many local residents as extras. ALVHS Archives

Jack London, with his dog Rollo, is shown in 1886 at age ten. As a boy he resided on a ranch near Livermore, attended school there, but was not terribly happy with his experience. Refer to recent writings of Janet Newton, available at the Livermore Heritage Guild or from the Amador-Livermore Valley Historical Society in Pleasanton. LHG Photo

William Mendenhall and his wife are shown in a happy mood as they apparently enjoy their own playing of the violin and accordion. Mendenhall is generally thought to be the founder of the city of Livermore, donating land and mapping the first portion of the town. ALVHS Archives

Aunt Lizzie Oliver came to Livermore in 1871. McLeod built the house where she lived, the street becoming known as Lizzie Street, now Livermore Avenue. She was born in West Virginia and died here in 1903. Legend has it that she was often seen wandering the streets picking up cigarette and cigar butts. Dopking Photo

To date this couple has not been identified, even though the Livermore Heritage Guild tried. It is interesting to note the almost universal severe expressions in photos of the late 1800s and early 1900s. LHG Photo

Pleasanton's Eilene Mohr was "Queen of the May" in 1913. May Day celebrations with Maypole dances were popular through the 1950s, especially in the elementary schools. ALVHS Archives

This group of men is not identified. There is the possibility they were turn-of-the-century policemen in Livermore. Dopking Photo

At a deer camp in 1932 in the hills of the south range near Sunol this group of ten hunters poses with ten deer obviously taken in the area. Moller Family Photo

A lodge group of men and women members from around the valley poses in Livermore. Moller Family Photo

Mathias Koopmann arrived in Dublin in the 1870s and is shown here with the Mein family (also from Germany) shortly after. The families lived together, sharing meager possessions. They are typical of the rural population, the mainstay of the valley economy for about a hundred years. ALVHS Archives

On October 18, 1910, the two families celebrated at the Koopmann's twenty-fifth anniversary at Hermanson Hall and Park in Palomares Canyon. Mr. and Mrs. Koopmann are pictured center. To the right in the photo are their six children. Mr. and Mrs. Mein are the other couple. Their four children are at the left. ALVHS Archives

Mr. and Mrs. Silvio Fiorio with sons
Charles and Frank and their dog Prince
in Livermore at the turn of the century.
ALVHS Archives, Lillie Fiori Photo

The Jacob Schneider family is pictured here in 1908. Top row (left to right) are John, Emma, Fredrick, and Lillie. In the front row are Margaret, Mary James (Graham), Gustav, and Jacob. The obvious connection with these two families is that Lillie Schneider married Charles Fiorio, the two settling in Pleasanton and operating Fiorio's Market on Rose Avenue. Their son Jack continued to run the store and meat cutting business until just recently. ALVHS Archives, Lillie Forio Photo

Posed in the yard of the Tehan home on Foothill Road near Dublin in the 1900s are Arlene Stewart Massey, Veronica Hilton Kiefer, and Dan Tehan. All are descendants of Jeremiah Fallon. ALVHS Archives

Behind Old St. Raymond's Catholic Church in Dublin is the well-tended cemetery which contains graves of the earliest residents of the west end of the Amador-Livermore Valley. Shown here is the Dougherty family plot and also the grave of Tom Donlon who was killed at age twenty-five while working on the roof of the church. Both a school and a street in Dublin are named after him. *Author Photos*

Standing in front of the Robert Livermore commemorative plaque in 1969 are co-chairmen for the Livermore Centennial Committee Paul Heppner (left) and Barry Schrader. The dedication to the first settler was by the Native Sons of the Golden West in 1935. LHG Photo

Celebrating Robert Livermore's memory in 1935 are seated (left to right) Charles Livermore, Kate Schenone, Victoria DiMartini, and Nicholas Livermore. LHG Photo

*And we must have a birthday party! The
Presbyterian Church Guild of Livermore
helps Mamie McCoy celebrate in the late
1930s. At the left is Anne McDonald. To
the right of Mamie are Barbara Wente
and Josephine Bernal. LHG Photo*

Dedications occur in all communities for many different reasons. Here is one to all men and women who gave their lives in service to their country. Pictured (left to right) at the base of this flagpole in Wayside Park in Pleasanton in the mid-1960s are Walt Lund, Rev. Byron Allender, Don Bowers, and John Rakestraw. Peter Bailey Photo, Author Collection

At the east end of Kottinger Park in Pleasanton on top of a hill on New Bernal Avenue is the Gary Meyer Memorial and Plaque. Shown here is Commander Robert Steffenauer of American Legion Post 237 and Auxiliary in 1969 presiding over the dedication to Gary, the first Pleasanton serviceman killed in action in Vietnam and to all who fought and gave their lives to defend human rights. Author Collection

A fitting close to this pictorial history is represented here as Justi Rogers, first president of the Amador-Livermore Valley Historical Society, poses with Walter and Margarietta Johnson on the occasion of their marriage (reception at Castlewood Country Club in 1965).

ALVHS was founded in 1963, a non-profit, volunteer organization dedicated to the preservation of historical sites and artifacts, the docu-mentation of the history of the valley, encouragement of community interest in the arts, and promotion of educational activities.

Mr. Johnson completely renovated the Agostin Bernal adobe on Foothill Road, adding to it to make a large residence and preserving it as a landmark. When finished, he had spent a reported $300,000 on the restoration and improvements. ALVHS Archives

Bibliography

BOOKS

Bennett, Virginia S. *Dublin Reflections (and bits of valley history)*. Union City: Mill Creek Press, 1978.

Brewer, William H. *Up and Down California in 1860-1864 (Ed. by F. P. Farquhar)*. Berkeley and Los Angeles: University of California Press, 1966 (New Edition).

Caughey, John W. *California*. Englewood Cliffs, N.J.: Prentice-Hall, Inc., 1953.

Davis, Dorothy, ed. *A Pictorial History of Pleasanton*. Pleasanton Bicentennial Committee, 1976.

Drummond, G. B. *A Guide to Architectural Styles in the Livermore-Amador Valley*. Union City: Mill Creek Press, 1978.

———. *Early Days in the Livermore-Amador Valley*. Alameda County School Department, 1973.

Kleinecke, Julia. *History of First Presbyterian Church Livermore, California*, 1871-1971. Livermore: 1971.

Mosier, Dan L. *Harrisville and the Livermore Coal Mines*. San Leandro: Road Books, 1978.

Newton, Janet. *Las Positas: The Story of Robert and Josefa Livermore*. Livermore: Janet Newton publisher, 1969.

———. *People, Bricks, and Timbers: The Story of St. Michael's Parish, Livermore, California*. Oakland: Spectrum West, 1978.

Stuart, Reginald and Grace. *Corridor Country*. Amador-Livermore Historical Society, 1966.

Thompson and West. *Official and Historical Atlas Map of Alameda County*. Fresno: Valley Publishers, 1976 (Bicentennial Print).

Wood, M. W. *History of Alameda County, California, 1883*. Oakland: Holmes Book Company, Reprinted 1969.

BOOKLETS AND PAMPHLETS

Delgado, James P. Sombras de la Noche, "The Augustin Bernal Adobe." San Jose: Smith and McKay Printing Co, 1976.

Doss, Ann. "Pleasanton (Architectural Styles)." ALVHS Museum, 1982.

Drummond, G. B. "Real Estate Development in Livermore History." Livermore Heritage Guild, 1979.

———. "Early Days of San Ramon and Dublin." (Reprint from Brown and Kauffman, 1966).

Hagemann, Herbert L., Jr. "Abstract of Title: Rancho El Valle de San Jose." (Reprint from May and August, *Pacific Historian*, 1965).

———. "Crane Ridge Lookout, 1931." Pleasanton Printers, 1976.

———. "Juan Pablo Bernal." *Pacific Historian*, VIII, Number 4 (Reprint).

McGown, J. E. "Progressive Pleasanton, 1902." The Pleasanton Times, 1902.

Mosier, Dan L. "The H. A. Coal Mine." San Leandro: Mines Road Books, 1979.

Newton, Janet. "Cresta Blanca and Charles Wetmore (A Founder of the California Wine Industry)." Livermore Heritage Guild, 1974.

———. "Jack London's Boyhood in Livermore." Livermore Heritage Guild, 1988.

———. "The Ravenswood Story." Livermore Heritage Guild, 1979.

Soito, Patricia. "A Hundred Years of Pleasanton (The Most Desperate Town of the West)." San Francisco: Phillips and Van Orden Co., 1949.

ARTICLES FROM NEWSPAPERS

Pleasanton Times, Livermore Herald, Stockton Record, Oakland Tribune, Independent, and the *Echo*.

Index

About the Authors

Bob and Pat Lane came to the Amador-Livermore Valley as newlyweds in June of 1952, straight out of college at the University of the Pacific, Stockton, California.

Bob put his then newly-acquired teaching credentials to work at Amador Valley High School through 1957, teaching English, journalism, yearbook, and drama. He then taught and served as a counselor for the next thirty years at Sunnyvale and Cupertino High Schools in the Santa Clara Valley. Retirement came in June of 1987. He has long been active in community organizations.

Pat became almost immediately involved in community activity and journalism, working as a correspondent, reporter, and editor at several valley newspapers until 1985 when she accepted the position of executive director of the Pleasanton Downtown Association and was also elected to the board of the Amador-Livermore Valley Historical Society. Bob and Pat have two sons and two grandchildren.

The authors' interest in the valley history and growth of local communities has come together in this volume.